DARKER THAN THE
DEEPEST SEA

DARKER THAN THE DEEPEST SEA

THE SEARCH FOR NICK DRAKE

TREVOR DANN

PORTRAIT

Visit the Portrait website!

PORTRAIT Portrait publishes a wide range of non-fiction, including
biography, history, science, music, popular culture and sport.

Visit our website to:
- read descriptions of our popular titles
- buy our books over the internet
- take advantage of our special offers
- enter our monthly competition
- learn more about your favourite Portrait authors

VISIT OUR WEBSITE AT: www.portraitbooks.com

Contents

Sweet spring, full of sweet dayes and roses
A box where sweets compacted lie
My musick shows ye have your closes
And all must die
George Herbert (1593–1633)
'Vertue'

I got to keep movin'
Blues fallin' down like hail
And these days keeps on worryin' me
There's a hellhound on my trail
Robert Johnson
Hellhound On My Trail (1937)

Il n'y a qu'un problème philosophique
vraiment sérieux: c'est le suicide
Albert Camus
The Myth Of Sisyphus (1942)

For Maureen, Celia and Henry

Introduction

NICK DRAKE wrote his own epitaph: no one knows the fruit tree, he sang, except the rain and air, but everyone will stand and stare when it's gone. Before he was 21 this handsome, privileged, gifted, English songwriter and guitarist had predicted that he would be unrecognised during his short life, but lauded long after he ended it, broke, alone, ignored, and ravaged by drugs.

The history of pop and rock music in the second half of the 20th century is littered with the corpses of musicians who couldn't cope either with fame or without it. Because he died by his own hand aged only 26, Nick Drake is usually filed alongside Kurt Cobain, Ian Curtis, Jim Morrison, Gram Parsons, Jeff Buckley, Tim Buckley and all the other promising-young-life-cut-short tragedies. But Nick's story is not the classic rock 'n' roll suicide or gonzo gross-out.

There has been no shortage of theories. And the evidence from people who knew him is often contradictory. He was an arrogant, spoiled, toffee-nosed, upper-class Hooray Henry who felt the world owed him a living and couldn't handle failure. Or he was a sensitive, over-protected child who

9

bravely broke away from his claustrophobic upper-class background, but never found the mental strength to deal with the pressures of the music business. He was charming company. He was withdrawn and aloof. He was gay. He had a series of passionate relationships with women. He couldn't face any sexual contact. His music is dreary, immature and self-pitying. He was one of the greatest guitarists who ever lived and his lyrics bear comparison with the works of Tennyson and Blake. He became mentally ill. He was a heroin user. He killed himself. He didn't kill himself. To borrow Winston Churchill's phrase, his life was 'a riddle wrapped in a mystery inside an enigma'.

Yet the debate about his music and his heritage rages with more intensity now than ever. When I embarked on this book in autumn 2004, a Google search revealed about 550,000 references to Nick Drake. Today there are over a million, far more than for Jeff Buckley (765,000) or Janis Joplin (625,000). There are six extravagantly detailed websites, including one in Italian, and several message boards. In the past few years there have been two TV documentaries, a BBC radio profile narrated by Brad Pitt, two new compilation CDs and even a promo video. He sold more records in 2004 than in any other year since his first album was released in 1969.

It's a measure of the growing appeal of Nick's music that even Hollywood has begun to embrace him. When a scene demands an atmospheric and introspective soundtrack, the call goes out for a Nick Drake song. Things Behind The Sun and One Of These Things First were used in *Garden State*

(2004), Black Eyed Dog and Cello Song in *The Good Girl* (2002), Northern Sky in *Serendipity* (2001), Fly in *The Royal Tenenbaums* (1999) and Road in *Hideous Kinky* (1998). The popular US television series *Young Americans* has also employed many of Nick's songs. It's the same in the compilation album business. In the first 15 years after his death Nick's music appeared on just one commercially available collection. In the subsequent 15 no less than 30 CDs have featured his songs. There is a growing number of cover versions too – many of the best of which, interestingly, have been by women vocalists, including Lucinda Williams (Which Will), Norma Waterson (River Man), Christine Collister (Black Eyed Dog) and Norah Jones (Day Is Done).[1] And in the UK, there's a fully fledged Nick Drake tribute act working the folk clubs and arts centres. Keith James, a guitarist and singer in his 50s, started his 'Songs Of Nick Drake' evenings to supplement his performances of his own songs. Now 'the Drake thing has almost taken over,' he told me, 'I could work every night of the year singing Nick's songs if I wanted to.'

There are even songs about Nick. The brilliant oddball singer-songwriter Robyn Hitchcock – like Nick, a former student at Cambridge University – recorded I Saw Nick Drake in 2002. Written on a barge as it slid silently down the Thames near Windsor, the song is a moving evocation of Nick's spirit with its arresting opening line, 'I saw Nick Drake on the corner of time and motion'. At an event held in Tanworth church to commemorate the 30th anniversary of Nick's death, the legendary Ashley Hutchings, who gave the young musician his big break in 1967, unveiled his new song about Nick called Given Time.[2] He explained that he began to write it soon after the radio and TV documentaries were aired in 2004. He couldn't sleep, thinking about the tragedy of Nick's short life and the part he had played himself in launching Nick's ill-starred career. 'Impossibly tall, incredibly still,' sang the now 60-year-old godfather of English folk music, 'he drew me closer against my will'. His musical partner Mark Hutchinson sang the closing lines about how some stars in the heavens will be 'brighter later'.

So what sets Nick Drake apart from the other pale, fey, introspective, angst-ridden shoe-gazers who have been thrown up by every generation and every musical movement in the UK?

The three albums released in his lifetime, a legacy of just 31 tracks, sound as fresh today as they did in the studio nearly 40 years ago – a great tribute to the work of Joe Boyd, their producer, and John Wood, the engineer at Sound Techniques in London. Whether augmented by a lavish string arrangement or a pumping rock band, or left alone with his guitar, Nick was able to create a unique and instantly recognisable sound – warm, crisp, immediate and utterly authentic – the perfect environment for his engaging, deceptively simple compositions.

Nick Drake was a sophisticated musician who could read and write music and knew the piano, the clarinet and the sax as well as he knew the guitar. He wasn't a folkie: he could play the folk club standards as well as anyone, but he didn't relate to the finger-picking acoustic tradition. Neither was he a typical teenage guitarist: he was interested in the fashionable experimentation of 1960s pop, but he didn't draw on the three-chord rock 'n' roll tradition either. His influences were avant-garde jazz, classical music, especially choral works, what we'd now call 'world music', and the blues. He played his acoustic guitar and used his narrow vocal range as though they were jazz instruments, weaving in and out of musical conventions, always experimenting with phrasing, tuning and time signatures to give his songs an unsettling, other-worldly feel. His vocals rarely start where we expect them. The emphasis in his lyrics rarely falls where rock or folk tradition would demand. He mixes major and minor chords with ease. He understands the modal compositional ideas of Miles Davis and avoids standard verse/chorus structures. Tony Reif, who produced the remarkable *Poor Boy* album,[3] which features jazz 'imaginings' of Nick's songs, says his compositions 'leave an aura of mystery hovering about them, like pieces of a puzzle that fit together perfectly even though the picture is never completed'. Reif believes it's their 'seductive ambiguity, always expressed within very precise musical structures that makes them so appealing to musicians'. And yet in spite of all this complex theory, the subtleties of Nick's compositions are easy to ignore. This may explain why his music has rarely found itself a home amid the oi!-listen-to-me pop tracks on radio playlists. As Robyn Hitchcock puts it, 'Nick Drake's music brushes the ear. The intentions may be dark, but the execution is light.'

In an era that prized the experimental (Hendrix), the fluent (Clapton) or the downright flash (Alvin Lee), Nick's guitar style went unnoticed by the mainstream. But guitarists who have tried to play his songs are quick to acknowledge the complexity and sheer virtuosity of his self-taught style. He laboured for hours to find tunings that would give his songs the settings he needed, often using chord shapes where the fifth and the octave are open strings, producing a distinctive drone. And he played with remarkable precision and an almost mechanical perfection. Most accomplished acoustic guitarists allow their instruments to buzz and whine as the fingers of their left hand race around the fret board hammering on and pulling off, but Nick's tone was always relentlessly clean and clear. Robert Smith of The Cure describes his technique as both 'impossible' and 'effortless'. Even on his favourite small-bodied Guild M20 he could produce a sound that would stop a college room conversation dead. Perhaps with modern stage equipment he would have been able to do the same in large theatres.

His lyrics are impressive too. To dismiss them as 'frozen in immaturity'[4] is to condemn Wilfred Owen for not being grown-up enough. Sure, most of Nick's words and ideas are those of a young man because they were mostly written before he was 24, but they are anything but simplistic and juvenile. When I asked Chris Bristow, Nick's old supervisor from Cambridge, to look at some of Nick's lyrics, he was fascinated. Reading the melancholic and prescient Fruit Tree, he said 'that seems to me like a combination of Blake and Tennyson in a way that I would hardly have believed possible. It has both the sadness of the idea that you are transient, from Tennyson, and the idea that you need to die to fruit, from Blake's "Songs Of Experience".' River Man reminded Bristow of Matthew Arnold's poem 'The River Of Life' and also of William Wordsworth's 'The Idiot Boy', which tells the story of a mother called Betty risking the life of her brain-damaged son to save the life of a friend. He also pointed out that Nick's phrasing was quintessentially English, not at all influenced by the Americanised style of most British songwriters of the time. So he was very literate, absorbed by the great English poets and by Baudelaire and Rimbaud who had first excited him during his gap year in Aix-en-Provence in 1967. But other critics have picked up on the more radical side of Nick's work and the influence of Jeremy Prynne and Sylvia Plath. There's more than a hint of waving and drowning in Nick's lyrics and Iain Cameron, who knew him at Cambridge and played flute on his final radio session, describes Nick's writing as 'a style that is taken from despair, not in the expectation that this will solve anything, rather that it will beautify and express estrangement and alienation'. Robyn Hitchcock picks up the same theme: 'It's a gentle doom that envelops the listener. There's a resignation at the bottom of it all. His songs are like butterflies attached to anchors.'

It's clear that once intrigued and beguiled by Nick Drake's music, many fans quickly develop an obsession for this elusive character. Reading the visitors' book in the parish church of Tanworth-in-Arden, the quaint English village where he lived and is buried, is at once an impressive and disturbing experience. Pilgrims who visit his grave from Australia, America, Italy, Greece, Finland, Japan and all over the world describe him as 'an angel', 'a prophet' and even 'a saviour'. On one of the Nick Drake message boards during 2005, someone wrote from the USA to compare Nick's status to that of the newly deceased Pope John-Paul II. From James Dean to Kurt Cobain, handsome creatives who die young have been canonised by succeeding generations, but with Nick there's something different. His movement is growing, not diminishing with the passage of time. He has more fans, more admirers, more worshippers as every year passes, so there must be something special about his music that continues to speak to people across the years. Of course the very things that prevented his career taking off – his shyness, his hatred of interviews, his reluctance to play live – now contribute to his enigma and encourage people to speculate about his motives or even invent their own details to fill in the gaps. Nick is so elusive, so mysterious, he's anything you want him to be.

1. A Soul with No Footprint

1. Cambridge

NICK DRAKE is tall and lean. He lives 'somewhere in Cambridge', somewhere close to the University (where he is reading English), ... does not have a telephone ... and tends to disappear for three or four days at a time...[5]

Nearly 40 years have passed since Vivien Holgate wrote Nick's first press release for Island Records in 1969 and he remains just as elusive in 21st-century Cambridge. Anyone searching for a blue plaque or a Beatles-style Magical History Tour will be sorely disappointed. And yet, apart from a few cosmetic changes – paved streets, a one-way traffic scheme, the ubiquitous Starbucks, Next and Gap – the town centre looks pretty much as it did when Nick arrived there, aged 19, in September 1967.

For the author Frederick Raphael, Cambridge was 'the city of perspiring dreams',[6] contrasting with Oxford, famously the city of dreaming spires. On a balmy summer's day as the punts meander gently along The Backs and the latest cohort of floppy-haired undergraduates fly along Trinity Street on their bicycles or spread out their picnic cloths and wine hampers on various college lawns, it's easy to fall in love with the romantic image of picture-postcard Cambridge. It's a different story in the winter when the icy horizontal winds blow in straight from the Urals and the trek across Midsummer Common feels like a polar expedition. But in every season Cambridge retains its unique ambience of chatter and culture, of high jinks and high art. Just to walk over the River Cam, along Garret Hostel Lane past Trinity Hall, where part of the 1981 movie *Chariots Of Fire* was filmed, up the ghostly cobbled Senate House Passage and on to King's Parade with the magnificent King's College Chapel looming over you is to feel the weight of 800 years of learning. Peeking through the massive medieval gates of some of the ancient colleges makes you want to pick up a book, any book, and read it there and then.

It's an environment that makes its own rules and delights in traditions that seem designed to confuse outsiders. The River Cam is always called the Granta as it flows through the heart of the old town. May Week, when the colleges hold their end-of-year balls, is actually a fortnight in June. Gonville & Caius College must be pronounced Gonville and Keys. Magdalene College is Maudlin. Autumn term is known as Michaelmas and a three-year degree course as the Tripos. To attend the university is to go up. To be expelled is to be sent down.

It was into this stimulating, forbidding setting that Nick Drake walked to study English. He was a striking youth, 6ft 3in tall, almost Adonis-like in his athletic grace and poise, coruscating when he smiled, sensuous, beguiling and just a little mysterious. When he spoke in his clipped, almost aristocratic way, he exuded self-assurance. But his contemporaries soon noticed that there was something impenetrable, intangible, about his character, as though if you reached out for him he'd be gone like the smoke of the Gauloises cigarette that invariably enveloped him.

Writers and fans alike have been quick to see the gothic grandeur of Cambridge architecture and the quiet atmosphere of reflection and study as a great influence on Nick's music, perhaps the place where his muse was nurtured. So it can be as big a shock for us, as it must have been for him, to see the place where his university career started. Like Oxford, Cambridge has no campus and no central administration block or student union building. The university runs the courses and confers the degrees, but it's the affiliated colleges, dotted all round the town, that recruit the students, house and feed them, and organise their individual teaching sessions (known as supervisions).

To find Nick Drake's college it's necessary to leave the architectural glories of the medieval city centre and head north past the famous Round Church, over the narrow Magdalene Bridge, and out into the bustle of real Cambridge. It's a walk that amply demonstrates the traditional divide between what's called town and gown. After climbing Castle Hill, the only incline of any note in the flatlands of East Anglia, you pass Cambridgeshire County Council's HQ, Shire Hall, before negotiating a sprawling five-way road junction at the beginning of Huntingdon Road. This is crowded enough now, but in 1967, before the M11 motorway and A14 dual carriageway were built, it was the main road from Harwich and the eastern ports to the midlands and north of England. Heavy lorries would thunder round the corner from Victoria Road and up towards Girton. Coming south their air brakes would squeal and pant as their gears ground together in readiness for a sharp left hand turn they hadn't expected.

A quarter of a mile past the junction, just where the lorries were at their noisiest is Fitzwilliam College, a monument to early 1960s functional design. A casual observer might assume that the three-storey grey-brick building with slit windows and a flat roof is an out-of-town distribution warehouse or perhaps an Ikea outlet. In fact, so anonymous is the building, designed by the celebrated British architect Sir Denys Lasdun, that when I arrived at Fitzwilliam, four years after Nick, to enrol as a history student, I asked a passer-by for directions. 'Is this some kind of student prank?' he huffed. I was standing right outside the main entrance.

Today, Fitzwilliam has doubled in size, taken over an adjacent mansion and its gardens, built a state-of-the art theatre and turned itself into a very attractive place to live and study. Its main entrance, or porters' lodge, is now on the quiet side of the College in stylish Storey's Way. And the lorries have gone, so students with rooms facing the main road don't have to fix plasticine to their window frames to stop them rattling. But in Nick's day and mine it was a soulless, ghastly place, a mile away from the beautiful heart of Cambridge and a millennium away from its medieval streets, tree-lined courts and cavernous bookshops. Joining Fitz was like booking three years at the Savoy only to find yourself allocated a room in the Slough Travelodge.

Like all first-year students, or freshers, in what was then an all-male college, Nick was allocated a college room. Later he would move into digs nearer the town, but his first experience of life as a Fitz Billy Boy was in room A2 on the ground floor at the back of the College, overlooking a car park. Today the room has been renamed P2 (room 2 on staircase P). Following the extensive building work in the 1990s, it's now right in the middle of the College, overlooking Tree Court and with an entrance off Fellows Court. The College doesn't officially admit visitors, but if you walk confidently past the porters' lodge you should be able to walk up to P block. Go straight on across Tree Court, through the gate into Fellows Court and turn immediately right.

From his vantage point on C staircase in 1967 (now renamed M) Nick's fellow English student John Venning would watch him come 'whizzing in and out of college'. His university friends Robert Kirby and Brian Wells also remember that he hated the room and spent as little time there as possible. Nick did his best to brighten up the white walls with fashionable flower-power posters, which he would buy cheaply in London and sell on at a profit to fellow undergraduates, but when his friend Victoria Ormsby-Gore visited him she found him 'crushed'. 'He just sat there saying "it's so awful". It was anathema to him. Torture.'[7]

The tiny rooms, each little bigger than a prison cell, were a hellish experience. While undergraduates in some of the older colleges often had two rooms, Fitzwilliam residents were squashed into a space about 6 metres square. There was a small built-in wardrobe, a desk and chair, a so-called easy chair covered in black leatherette and, along one of the long walls, a padded cupboard and shelf unit designed for the single bed to fit underneath to create a settee. This arrangement presupposed that the inhabitant was up early enough to allow his bedder (cleaning lady) to get in, make the bed and roll it back for daytime use. In reality most students pushed their beds to another wall so they could sleep at any time during the day. And if anyone did try to use the bed as a settee, they were dicing with death. The floor was helpfully covered in shiny lino tiles so a hapless guest leaning back on the padded cupboard could make the bed fly across the room on its castors. At the end of the room facing the door was a large floor-to-ceiling picture window, a nightmare in a ground-floor room with no net curtains or blinds. Like many Fitz students before and since, Nick liked to keep his curtains closed whenever he was in residence.

Along the corridor was the gyp room, or kitchen, two toilets and a bathroom, all of which Nick shared with his colleagues on the ground floor of A staircase – CA Fergusson (A1), CJ Hughes (A3), NN Salmon (A4) and EB Gilchrist (A5) – not that they would have seen much of him. From the outset, Nick exuded a sense of belonging somewhere else. Everyone who met him felt he was just passing through. He didn't connect with Fitzwilliam at all. The NR Drake gazing out from the second to back row of the official 1967 college matriculation photograph looks sullen and unimpressed. His hair is long by 1967 university standards, roughly Beatles 1965 length, and the tie is slackened just enough to suggest polite rebellion.

It wasn't just the room. As a new college Fitzwilliam hadn't had time to develop much of an academic reputation. But it was keen on sport and the Master, Dr WW Grave, was determined to raise the College profile by winning some university silverware. So a large proportion of Nick's colleagues were cricketers, rugby players and rowers, not his kind of people at all. Victoria Ormsby-Gore recalled him complaining that 'When these people say come out and get stoned, they mean go the pub and get drunk!'[8] Alcohol was not Nick Drake's drug of first choice.

Brian Wells, then a medical student at Selwyn College, was sitting with Nick in A2 one afternoon listening to Van Morrison's *Astral Weeks*. 'We were smoking a joint and suddenly these feet started appearing at the top of the window and it was the guys upstairs who were sitting on their window ledge kicking their feet and we were both stoned and Nick goes, "Wow look, weird" ... they were the rugger buggers and we were the cool people smoking dope.' On more than one occasion Nick had words with Chris Hughes about the rowdy friends he brought back to A3 next door.

Like all Cambridge students Nick was assigned a tutor to look after his welfare. Dr Ray Kelly is a bluff Yorkshireman who taught French and took the role of being *in loco parentis* very seriously. He is a warm and engaging man, not in the least authoritarian, who remembers Nick very well to this day, although at the time he sensed he was being kept at a distance. 'I never felt that I'd got through to him,' he says. 'He was pleasant but beyond reach, beyond my reach anyway.' Did the College authorities know or care about Nick's drug use? 'Well it was a concern,' says Ray, 'but he came over as shy, not withdrawn. We were worldly wise and we knew what to look out for and what to smell, but it never occurred to me that he might have been doing more than other people.'

As the lyrics to his earliest songs testify, Nick liked to cast himself in the role of observer rather than participant. In some ways the Fitzwilliam experience forced his hand because he found himself out of step with the majority of students. There's no doubt, however, that he enjoyed cultivating an air of mystery. He liked to 'creep around', says one contemporary at Fitzwilliam. Another, Dave Punter, now Professor of English at Bristol University, remembers being 'not frightened exactly but distantly impressed' by this 'tall, good-looking, rather dreamy' boy. He told fellow student, John Venning, who can now be found running the English Department at the prestigious St Paul's School in London, that Nick was 'one to watch'.

John Venning tells one particular story that evokes Nick's demeanour during his early months at university. Once a week he and Nick would attend supervisions with a young postgraduate called Chris Bristow. They were held in an attic room at the top of a rambling old house at 9 West Road in Cambridge, a site now occupied by the hideous salmon-pink and steel building that houses the English Faculty.[9] 'I arrived quite early one day and either it was raining or for some reason I went indoors to sit on the old servants' staircase and wait. And I found that Nick was already there. And I took to coming earlier and earlier but Nick was always there before I was. I thought this was really strange. There was Nick on the stairs looking out of this garret window, just like on the cover of *Five Leaves Left*. I kept turning up to see when he turned up. I just thought it was really strange that he was there earlier and earlier and I never solved the mystery.' Chris says, 'I used to suspect that Nick had slept there overnight!' More probably Nick was going straight to West Road from Cambridge railway station, having spent the night in London. From the beginning, and certainly from his second term onwards, Nick had far more pressing things on his mind than the 19th-century poetry and prose he was meant to be studying. His older sister Gabrielle was beginning to make her name as an actress after studying at the Royal Academy of Dramatic Art and Nick would travel to London regularly to stay in her flat on Prince of Wales Drive in Battersea. From there he was close to the Chelsea homes of a group of socialites and debutantes he'd met while studying French during his gap year. Hanging out with them, smoking dope and discussing Rimbaud and Verlaine was a lot more fun than attending lectures and supervisions in Cambridge. 'Nick didn't do any work; he never did any work,' says Brian Wells. 'At that time in Cambridge you could sail through without going to lectures; you didn't have to write essays, all you had to do was scrape through exams. I vividly remember an occasion where we were having tea with people, cooking crumpets on these gas fires with metal forks, and it was six weeks before exams and this other guy said he'd already done his revision and Nick and I were gobsmacked.'

At Chris Bristow's weekly supervisions, Nick was uncommunicative. 'You always knew he was pretty bright but I couldn't mobilise him very well. I couldn't get him into an area where he'd be enthused enough to do a serious week's work. He was clever enough to do a minimal amount of work and write a minimalist essay that was just enough. He had to be bright to be coasting like that.' John Venning couldn't penetrate Nick's studied air of cool: 'I tried to talk with Nick, the way you would to someone who was your supervision partner. You know, "Have you done your essay, have you done your reading" or whatever, and I got very little back, very little. And in Chris's supervisions for the entire term Nick hardly said a word. It almost became a one-on-one between myself and Chris, with Nick as a sort of presence in the space.' It's easy to imagine Nick hunched up in a corner of the supervision room, wearing the enigmatic, slightly supercilious smile he adopted, and wondering just what he was doing in the company of people who were conventional enough to think that studying and writing essays was important.

To borrow his great fan Clive Gregson's words, Nick had 'lost himself to the guitar'. According to Ed Gilchrist, an engineering student who lived on the same corridor, Nick 'sat in his room playing guitar all the time. He was obsessed with it. If you met him in the kitchen or popped into his room for a chat he wouldn't talk about anything else'. When he was in his room you could hear his endless tuning and retuning day and night, always in small fragments, never complete songs. Occasionally he would sing or hum wordless melodies as new songs took shape behind the colourful Hendrix poster that adorned the door of A2.

Even if Nick had given Cambridge a chance, it would probably have let him down. 'An awful lot of people didn't go to lectures. The quality of them was extremely variable,' says John Venning. Fitzwilliam College had organisational problems too. Norman Walters, its Director of Studies in English, who had recruited Nick, had died suddenly in the summer of 1967. His successor, Dominic Baker-Smith, found that 'we had too many undergraduates and all the plans were in Walters' head'. Even a self-confessed swot like John Venning was quickly frustrated. 'The College has never fully supported English. There was no coherence among the year – I don't think we were ever all gathered together to meet each other. English undergraduates at Fitz were very disgruntled.'

In fact students were pretty disgruntled about everything in 1967 and 1968. The notorious Garden House riot and Greek Week didn't happen until 1970 but this was already the era of sit-ins and protest marches. Prime Minister Harold Wilson was threatened when he appeared at Cambridge Guildhall in 1967, and the following year radical Fitzwilliam students hung a huge banner around the fluted windows of the College dining hall bearing the popular slogan of the time 'What we have here is a failure to communicate.'[10] John Venning remembers some 'nasty confrontations' with the 'paternalistic, old school' members of the College who wanted it run on traditional lines and rejected the new radical ideas of the time.[11]

Yet Nick Drake seems to have been oblivious to all this excitement. Arguably one of the reasons his music has lasted so long is that it was never contemporary. He wasn't concerned with the superficialities of the moment. What interested him were the timeless truths and the deepest emotions of life. And getting stoned. A lot.

Unsurprisingly Nick ended his first academic year at Cambridge with very poor results. The university awards its brightest students a 'first'. Most of the rest get what's called a 2:1 or a 2:2, a second-class mark divided into two categories. In his prelim exams, taken in May 1968, Nick was awarded a third, the lowest pass. His best mark was in French translation, his worst in 'Literature From 1625 to 1798', where his report records 'short work', often a euphemism for 'couldn't be bothered to finish and walked out for a fag'.

His college supervision reports paint a similar picture. Chris Bristow's, dated March 1968, is priceless: 'A Mona Lisa smile seems to be the main stock-in-trade; what's going on behind it I have little means of knowing. Nothing possibly, although I suppose a mind is at work in the few thin essays

I've had from him. There may be personal reasons for this lack of industry, but I haven't been able to find any. Could it be sloth?' The Chaucerian scholar Maurice Hussey wrote 'it has taken a month of extremely dull essays to reach the point at which he has begun to show a little vitality and intellectual initiative'. Joan Blake, who supervised Nick on Shakespeare reported that 'Mr Drake has been a disappointing student. He tends to be a sleeping partner and contributes little to discussion. He seems to find difficulty in expressing orally the character of his response to the texts set and this is confirmed by his written work which, though punctual and adequate in length, is vague, rather scrappy and invariably inconclusive.'

Ian Wright, reporting on Nick's work on 18th-century literature found the same. 'Still very immature essay style,' he wrote in the summer of 1968, 'very much 6th form type of work, rather verbose, rather "literary", rather afraid to commit itself. He's obviously interested in literature and is trying hard but does not exhibit very much originality of thought yet – his essays tend to be a weighing up of other critics' opinions. Also, they don't cover enough ground. This all sounds pretty damning, but isn't meant to; he has the necessary capacity for sensitive, personal response, and for original and forceful formulation but doesn't use them ... Probably needs to work harder too.'

What none of these academics, and few of his friends, knew was that Nick was actually working extremely hard, though not on his English course.

2. The Roundhouse

IT USED to be thought that Nick Drake was discovered, almost accidentally, during his time at Cambridge and that he was dragged kicking and screaming down to London and turned into a reluctant recording artist. But this handsome, polite and reserved 19-year-old was no shrinking violet. It's now clear that at the very time he was pledging three years of his life to university, he was already pursuing his musical ambitions and looking for a way to develop a career as a singer-songwriter. Chris Blackwell, founder and boss of Island Records, has a vivid recollection of Nick making an appointment to see him in late 1967 at Island's head office in Basing Street, West London, and bringing in a demo tape of his own compositions. These must have been the songs that have emerged on the so-called 'work tape', released posthumously on a number of bootleg albums. Time Has Told Me, Time Of No Reply and The Thoughts Of Mary Jane are likely to have been among them. 'I liked him very much,' says Chris Blackwell. 'He was shy but quite confident, nothing like he became later.' They sat together in Blackwell's office and listened to the tape. 'The songs had a frailty, a vulnerability that really pulled you in. I didn't have any doubt he'd be big some time.' But there would be no contract this time round. The only similar act on Island was John Martyn, whose first album, *London Conversation*, had just been released and Blackwell didn't think the recording had done Martyn justice. 'We were more into rock – Spooky Tooth, Traffic, bands like that – so I told him we didn't really have the expertise to produce him. I asked him to come back in six or eight months.'

A few weeks afterwards, just before Christmas 1967,[12] Nick found himself on the bill at a five-day benefit event in one of London's most prestigious rock venues. Situated in Chalk Farm, just half a mile from the Belsize Park flat that Nick would move to in 1969, the Roundhouse had been built as a turntable for steam trains in the 19th century. But by the late 1960s it had become a regular venue for happenings, freak-outs and all-nighters featuring underground acts of the time, notably Pink Floyd. Quite what this particular event, organised by an organisation called Circus Alpha Centauri, was benefiting, and how Nick came to be playing there are unclear. It's possible that the connection was James Fraser, vocalist with the band 117, who knew both Nick and Mick Jagger's brother Chris, who was a regular fixer at underground events in the capital. What we do know is that top of the bill were Country Joe & The Fish, making their British debut with one set on Wednesday December 20th and two sets the following night. In *Melody Maker*'s review of the festival, published January 6, 1968, in its 'Caught In The Act' column, there is no mention of any of the support acts, just an outline of the Country Joe & The Fish set, mainly taken from their albums *Electric Music For The Mind And Body* and *I Feel Like I'm Fixin To Die*, plus a long moan about the distorted sound in the cavernous Roundhouse with a plea for 'modern groups' to improve the 'general quality of their amplification'. As a flavour of the period it may be worth adding that on the opposite page, the *Melody Maker*'s review of The Beatles' *Magical Mystery Tour*, just aired on BBC TV, declared that hostile newspaper articles 'show the gap between the today people and suburbia'.

Just how many of the today people were still awake or conscious when Nick Drake took to the stage at the Roundhouse in the small hours of that December night, it's difficult to say. But one of them was certainly paying attention. Ashley Hutchings, later to become known as the 'Godfather of English Folk Music', was the bass player in Fairport Convention, then an American-influenced rock outfit, who had played a set earlier in the evening. With no defined backstage area or dressing rooms at the Roundhouse, performers mingled with the crowd and often sat on the floor to watch other acts. Hutchings was wandering through the venue when he found himself 'drawn to the stage by this very hypnotic sound'. He remembers two people playing, 'someone seated, a second guitar probably, and this very tall, very upright figure standing up.[13] I was drawn to his aura – although he didn't move much I felt he was magnetic.' This was an unexpected treat in the bare and dusty Roundhouse. 'The guitar playing was very accomplished, but there were no freaky or extended solos. This was the era for long songs and non-songs, but this was different. These were melodic, literate songs. I was spellbound.'

When the set ended Hutchings made his way to the side of the stage and found the mysterious singer-songwriter. 'I said, "I'm Ashley Hutchings from Fairport Convention", and he said "Oh ..., er, Nick Drake, pleased to meet you." I found him friendly and open, and I asked him did he want to get on, was he interested in recording. He said yes, very positively, and we exchanged phone numbers. Next day I contacted our manager Joe Boyd and said "you really must hear this guy".' Suddenly Nick Drake was in the best address book in town.

Joe Boyd was the Jack Kennedy of the UK music business. Folk guitarist and friend of Led Zeppelin, Roy Harper, remembers that people used to go quiet when the suave and quietly spoken American would sweep into the famous cellar of Les Cousins folk club in Soho. 'Here is,' they'd whisper, 'the next President of the United States!' His reputation was formidable. Born in 1942 in Boston, Massachusetts, he had been production manager at the famous Newport Folk Festival when Dylan went electric, tour manager for Muddy Waters and, from 1965, the London-based ambassador for the highly influential Elektra Records. He was one of the founders of the UFO (Underground Freak Out) Club, which was at the epicentre of 'swinging' London, and had produced the earliest recordings by both Soft Machine and Pink Floyd. In 1966 he founded his own production and management company, Witchseason, a name inspired by the Donovan song Season

Of The Witch, and later matched it with Warlock, a song-publishing company. On his roster in 1968 were the weird and wonderful Incredible String Band, the acoustic duo John And Beverley Martyn, and Fairport Convention, featuring vocalist Sandy Denny and guitarist Richard Thompson. Most impressively Joe Boyd must have taken his portrait to the attic. Even now, well into his 60s, he could still pass for no more than 40 years old.

Joe Boyd's role in Nick's story is difficult to over-estimate, and the relationship between the two men is pivotal in this ultimately tragic tale. In the early years, Nick's story was largely told by Joe, so for a long time he was seen as Nick's mentor, a brilliant and tenacious operator who nevertheless found time to nurture and support a young man whose talent he admired and wanted to bring to a wider public. And, to be fair, any criticism of Joe Boyd's management of Nick's career must be seen in the context of the artist's non-participation in nearly everything he was asked to do. Peter Jenner, who took over the management of Pink Floyd from Joe, says that he wouldn't have touched Nick 'with a bargepole'. So it is to Joe Boyd's credit that he took a risk on this unknown and difficult artist, and offered him the opportunity to fulfil his potential. In recent years, however, some critics have been less kind to Joe, seeing Nick as exploited and ultimately abandoned, eaten up and spat out by a voracious entrepreneur. It is certainly arguable that Nick's health and his self-image, as well as his chances of success, might have improved if he hadn't fallen under the Witchseason spell. But in 1968, for 19-year-old Nick Drake to have an 'in' with such an influential transatlantic figure as Joe Boyd was a huge break.

After a brief telephone call from Nick to set up a meeting, their relationship began when Nick turned up at the Witchseason offices at 83 Charlotte Street, London W1, with a reel-to-reel tape recorded at his home. He had been working on some new recordings during the Christmas holiday and presented Joe with four tracks: Time Of No Reply, I Was Made To Love Magic, Time Has Told Me and (probably) The Thoughts Of Mary Jane. Joe was captivated. 'One thing that was appealing about it was that it was not reaching out to you. In a way he was almost playing to himself. He wasn't trying to get you interested, he just was playing for his satisfaction. The other thing that was quite unique, and you could hear it on those demos, was the guitar playing. It was really strong, really deceptive. He wasn't flashy, he didn't show off. It wasn't like John Martyn or Robin Williamson, doing very clever things on the guitar so you noticed right away.'[14] Joe listened to the tape over and over again and became convinced that this young singer-songwriter with no fan base, no reputation on the live circuit and no recording experience might be worth a punt.

* * *

MEANWHILE in Cambridge on a brisk spring evening just before Easter 1968, a small ensemble gathered in the beautiful wood-panelled Bateman Room tucked away in the corner of Gonville & Caius College. Frantically studying the sheet music they had been handed moments earlier, a string quartet, two flautists and a double bassist were taking last-minute instructions from the French horn player, who was trying to tune everyone to a bright red Farfisa compact combo organ. Crouched over a reel-to-reel TRD tape recorder in a massive wooden box, the recording engineer looked up at the large stereo microphones hanging from the ceiling and gave a thumbs-up. After much shuffling and throat-clearing a tall, slim and elegant young man wrapped himself round an acoustic guitar and settled into a small wooden chair. He squinted at the 60 or so fellow students seated on the floor. He looked down at his zip-up boots. Then in a clipped, slightly hesitant and rather upper-class voice he whispered, 'This first song is one called Time Of No Reply.' The recording career of Nick Drake had begun.

'It was crap,' says Robert Kirby, who had organised the session and written the parts for the musicians. 'The problem was a lot of the string players followed Nick's vocal – they weren't used to somebody singing two or three beats later than the guitar rhythm. It was all over the place.' Colin Fleetcroft, who played the double bass, can't recall the event at all. 'I'd never heard of Nick Drake until the 1990s when my nephew told me I was mentioned in a book about him and took me into a record shop to see his CDs!' But Peter Rice, who recorded the gig, was 'mesmerised. The singer was a bag of nerves and there were some mistakes but the quality of the songs shone through.' Peter went home with the tape and tried to learn the guitar chords to one of the songs, a wistful piece he noted on the box as Made To Love Magic.

You can see the outside of the Bateman Room, scene of this historic concert, from Senate House Passage, just round the corner from King's College Chapel in the centre of Cambridge. It was altered during the 1990s to make way for a new auditorium but most of it is still standing. To the north side of the cobbled alleyway is Gonville & Caius College and halfway along you'll see a stone arch called the Gate of Honour. The three pairs of narrow mullioned windows to its left run the length of the Bateman Room, which Robert Kirby describes fairly as like 'a small old-fashioned parish hall'. That's where the blue plaque should go.

Robert Kirby's meeting with Nick Drake may not be quite as significant as the famous encounter between John Lennon and Paul McCartney at the Woolton village fete ten years earlier, but it was a seminal moment in both their careers and Robert is undoubtedly one of the heroes of the Nick Drake story. Pictures from the time show him with fashionably long hair, wire-framed glasses and corduroy flares. While Nick was still developing as an instrumentalist, Robert was already an accomplished musician and had been in a folk band since he was 14, touring Europe and recording. He went up to Cambridge in 1967 not only as a music student but also as a choral exhibitioner,[15] which meant singing in Caius chapel six days a week, including twice on Wednesdays and Sundays. On Mondays the choristers wore black robes and sang plainchant by candlelight.

Robert and Nick first met in September 1967 when they both auditioned for the prestigious Cambridge revue group The Footlights, whose past members had included Alan Bennett, Jonathan Miller, Peter Cook, David Frost and John Cleese. Given the overwhelming evidence of Nick's shyness at Cambridge it's remarkable that once again, when he was motivated, he could cast off the diffidence and throw himself into situations that took considerable courage. Here he was in his very first week at university appearing at a smoker[16] in front of a panel that included Clive James, Jonathan James-Moore and possibly Germaine Greer. Sadly neither Nick nor Robert were selected, which is a pity because it would have been interesting to see either of them on stage with Pete Atkin, Julie Covington and Rob Buckman in the 1968 show *Supernatural Gas*. Or perhaps not.

Robert returned to his elegant college rooms – Q4 on the first floor of Tree Court in Caius[17] – and concentrated on his other musical activities with The Gentle Power of Song, a choral group that was sometimes known as Fab Cab.[18] This group was run by the affable Marcus Bicknell, also a Caius student, who would nowadays be described as a networker. His mother, Marie, ran the Cambridge Ballet Workshop for children and when she needed some expert help with the sound cues for a show taking place in Bury St Edmunds, Bicknell put her in touch with another college acquaintance Peter Rice, who was president of the Cambridge University Tape Recording Society. When this was a success, Rice was invited to record demo tapes of GPOS, which resulted in them being offered a recording contract. So it was quite natural for Robert Kirby to approach Peter Rice with another project. 'He asked me if I could record some arrangements he'd done for a promising singer-songwriter called Nick Drake. I'd never heard of him,' says Peter. Robert Kirby remembers being contacted by James Fraser, the music scholar at Caius who may have arranged for Nick to play at the Roundhouse. Fraser had told Kirby about a friend who was looking to enhance his acoustic guitar songs with string parts.

Robert Kirby agreed to a meeting and Nick came to Q4 one afternoon with his Guild M20 guitar and a book of lyrics. 'It was absolutely stunning,' Kirby told a Belgian radio reporter. 'I was working a lot with classical musicians, and [Nick's] was virtuoso playing. He did not make mistakes. To start with I thought the voice was a bit weak, but that was just my immaturity. I soon saw it was the perfect way to deliver the lyrics and vocals of those songs, very understated.'[19] Shortly afterwards Nick wrote home quite excitedly. 'My musical friend, a guy named Robert Kirby, is working quite hard on arrangements for some of my songs and seems to be pretty competent. He's a rather splendid fellow and looks rather like Haydn or Mozart or someone, being rather short and stocky with long wavy hair and rimless spectacles. However he's quite hip to my kind of music being quite a proficient folk singer himself.'[20]

Nick and Robert had a lot in common. They could both read and write music, not a common skill in the rock and folk worlds, and they had similar musical tastes, from acoustic guitar pickers like Bert Jansch and Davy Graham through Randy Newman to classical composers like Bach, Debussy and Ravel. From the outset they trusted each other. Nick was not a natural collaborator, but he sensed that Robert Kirby would deliver the settings he imagined for his songs. It was the results of these early collaborations between Nick and Robert that were premiered in the Bateman Room. Marcus Bicknell played flute, a law student called Edward Bailey was on cello, Colin Fleetcroft played double bass and various friends of Robert's made up the rest of the ensemble. As well as Time Of No Reply and I Was Made To Love Magic, the group stumbled their way through three other original compositions, introduced by Nick. 'Now I'm not quite sure what's going to happen in this number. It's called My Love Left With The Rain'; 'This is one, it's called The Thoughts Of Mary Jane'; 'This is one arranged for string quartet. It's called Day Is Done.'

In 2004, after watching the documentary film *A Skin Too Few* on television, Peter Rice, now a partner in a successful electronic design company, wondered if he might still have a copy of his old tape. He knew the original had gone to Robert Kirby, but he thought he might have kept a quarter-track 7½ i.p.s. copy. He searched the loft of his house near Cambridge and amazingly there it was, nearly 40 years old, but still safe in its box. Peter's biggest problem was finding an ancient domestic four-track tape machine to play it on, but he eventually tracked one down for £30 via eBay and, after lacing up the tape with some trepidation, found that it still played. He knew he was in possession of a significant musical treasure. Visitors to the 30th Anniversary Concert held at Nick's birthplace in 2004 were treated to some extracts from the spoken introductions to the songs, but sadly at the time of writing there are no plans for the performances themselves to be released on record by Nick's estate.

We'll never know whether Nick himself would have sanctioned the release of the Bateman Room concert. We do know, however, that he was very pleased with it at the time. So much so that he was soon in contact with Peter Rice to arrange more recordings, this time solo. In his college pigeonhole a few days later, Peter found a note from Nick telling him that he needed a new demo tape of his songs and asking if Peter could bring his recording equipment up to Fitzwilliam College. Even in those comparatively traffic-free days, students weren't normally allowed to keep cars, but Peter Rice had successfully applied to the quaintly named University Motor Proctor's office for permission to keep a minivan to transport the Tape Recording Society's and his own equipment. So he loaded it up and drove round to Storey's Way at the appointed time.

'Unfortunately,' says Peter, 'it took several goes to get him to be in a suitable state to do any recording. One Saturday or Sunday morning he hadn't got any clothes on and he clearly had company as well, female company, two females in fact, so it wasn't the time.' On another occasion he 'opened the door and I could hear men's voices inside and a waft of aroma came out'. We can assume Peter Rice is not talking about aftershave. When he did finally get his microphones set up in Fitzwilliam, Nick wasn't on his best form. 'He kept buzzing strings and his vocals were poor, so when I got the tape back to my room I remember shaking my head and thinking "This is not on." There was nothing there that I could really salvage, even by splicing different takes together, so I eventually contacted him and said, "Sorry we're going to have to do it again." I think he'd realised.' The acoustics in Nick's tiny college room didn't help either. 'I was listening on headphones. What I didn't know was permeating it was a low rumble from an extractor fan and there was a blackbird joining in during one of the better takes. I think I used the same tape again. It wasn't even worth keeping and a reel of tape was expensive, the equivalent of about 25 pints of beer!'

They agreed to try again in more agreeable surroundings. Peter had a friend who was a scholar at Peterhouse, one of the traditional city-centre colleges. His status gave him a suite of very swanky rooms, which Peter negotiated to borrow one weekend when his friend was away. 'I set up the recorder and speakers in the bedroom and the microphones in the sitting room. Nick shambled in and we had a long discussion about microphone technique because one of the things I was dissatisfied with on the Fitzwilliam recordings was that I had the mics as a stereo pair and it wasn't a particularly good sound. He was too far away and the sound was bouncing off the white walls. Nick said, "What would it sound like if we did it the other way round?" So I said, "Well I'll play the guitar and attempt to sing", and we mic'd it up so there was one mic near the guitar and one for the vocal. These were SDC4038s, the big BBC jobs, very good mics for what they were designed for, distance mics, but not for close-up work. I had Nick's guitar and played it and I remember the tuning – I was used to a bottom D instead of an E but I wasn't used to an F sharp instead of a G – anyway I managed to play something and he came out of the control room shaking his head and he said, "No really, it's got to be a stereo pair."' This gave the recordings what Peter Rice calls 'a roomy sort of acoustic' but it was what Nick prescribed. 'He wanted it to sound like it would to someone who was sitting in the audience, not to a recording engineer. He preferred a more ambient sound.' As he was tidying up in the bedroom/control room Peter Rice called out, 'Well what do you think of that, Nick? Nick? … Nick?' He'd gone without saying goodbye.

In typically mysterious fashion, Nick hadn't been forthcoming about why he wanted the demo tape, but as the Peterhouse session ended he had confided in Peter Rice that it was required urgently by a top man in the London music business. Peter sat up late into the night with a razor blade, splicing the tape and transferring the best takes on to small spools so that, in those days before cassettes were in popular use, they could be played on a domestic tape machine. The finished 15 i.p.s. recording consisted of solo versions of the five songs from the Bateman Room concert plus two or three new ones, and lasted about half an hour. Peter Rice wrote a note saying 'Rewind carefully, the splicing tape's a bit old!' and put the reels in a parcel, which he delivered to Fitzwilliam College.[21]

There would be a long gap, however, before the initial contacts between Nick and Witchseason would turn into the release of his first album. By the time Peter Rice's recordings had arrived on Joe Boyd's desk it was exam season. Nick might not have been the most assiduous worker, but he had to spend some time in college or he would be sent down. And in those days the age of majority was still 21 so his parents would have to sign any paperwork, and his father Rodney in particular was unlikely to look kindly on any distraction from the university course.

Eventually, however, during the long summer vacation of 1968, a contract was signed. By today's standards it would be seen as shamefully exploitative, Joe Boyd taking the roles of manager, agent, song publisher and record producer. Conflict of interest wasn't a familiar expression in the music business of the time and in the excitement of signing a deal, Nick and his parents may not have considered what might happen if he ever needed a manager to renegotiate his record or publishing deals or a record company to support his live gigs. Nick knew little about the financial and legal sides of the industry. He simply wanted to be looked after by someone who could make things happen. And by a happy coincidence

Witchseason's latest licensing deal was with Chris Blackwell's Island Records, so Nick would become a member of the coolest roster in the UK alongside Jethro Tull, Traffic, Free and Bob Marley. Best of all he would get £10 a week spending money on top of his student grant.

3. *Five Leaves Left*

FROM THE autumn of 1968 Nick Drake began to live a double life. Like the infamous Cambridge spies of an earlier age, he was dividing his time between the student world and something all together more glamorous and subversive. He was well practised at hiding secrets, so as far as his university contemporaries and the College authorities were concerned, he was simply a shy boy who would occasionally disappear to London. One of the attractions of Cambridge for generations of students has been its proximity to the capital, now just 45 minutes by train to King's Cross and in the 1960s only just over an hour down the old line to Liverpool Street station. Cambridge students Pete Atkin and Clive James, captured the mood in their song for Footlights, Girl On A Train, which appeared on their first album in 1971: 'What did I do yesterday, well I'll tell you in brief, ten quid from the bank and I got out of town with relief.'

Like most Fitzwilliam undergraduates Nick was allocated digs for his second year. In October 1968 he moved into a small bedroom in Handley Villa, a terraced Victorian artisan's cottage at 56 Carlyle Road, now the office of The Spaulding Trusts. Situated on a quiet residential street, it had the benefit of being nearer the centre of Cambridge, but it meant living with an old-fashioned landlady who had little patience with Nick's lifestyle. So after prolonged negotiations with his college he was eventually allowed to move into one of four rooms in a nearby lodging house owned by Trinity College. Along the street from the flat where his musical collaborator Robert Kirby's girlfriend used to live, 65 Chesterton Road overlooks the River Cam as it passes Jesus Green on its way to the famous university boathouses. It's often been suggested that Nick's regular to-ing and fro-ing across the old iron bridge over the Cam was the inspiration for River Man, but Robert confirms that Nick was rarely seen in either of his digs and was more regularly found in his own room in town, on the ground floor of 25 Green Street, just round the corner from the famous Cambridge landmark The Whim.[22]

Indeed Nick spent such a lot of time with Robert Kirby, James Fraser, Mike Schützer-Weissman, Peter Russell, Chris Jones, Paul Wheeler and his other new friends at Gonville & Caius College that he was invited to join a curious and now-defunct society called The Loungers. Membership was normally restricted to Caius students, but one undergraduate from another college was invited annually to be their 'oddefellowe'. In 1968 this was Drake NR from Fitzwilliam, who was handed a Loungers membership card written in mock medieval English:

Ye Ancient Order of Gonville Loungers
10 elected members, must be voted in by all.
Committee of three, president, secretary and Oddefellowe
Must lounge at the gate of humility once a week at 1pm
for 5 minutes and 'obferve how ftrange creatures
ye Lord hath made'
Must wear loungers tie once a week
Fine of one crown for all breaches and conduct
unbecoming
A meale of immenfe fplendoure for Ye Loungers in
Mayye Weeke.

Peter Rice has a clear memory of Nick lounging against the wall at the Gate of Humility on Trinity Street, the main entrance to Caius, and chatting animatedly with Jeremy Prynne, the English academic and highly regarded modern poet, now Professor JH Prynne. At the other end of the literary spectrum Nick and Paul Wheeler went to lounge with the 89-year-old EM Forster in his rooms at King's College, where they discussed *Howards End* and *A Passage To India* over tea and biscuits.

Much lounging time was dedicated to listening to records. Paul Wheeler remembers the group enjoying 'an extraordinary eclectic range of music' from the American jazz pianist Jaki Byard and the Dutch harpsichordist and early music expert Gustav Leonhardt to Smokey Robinson and Brian Wilson. Nick particularly enjoyed Randy Newman's I Think It's Going To Rain Today, Tim Buckley's mystical Morning-Glory and The Steve Miller Band's dope-infused instrumental Song For Our Ancestors from their *Sailor* album. But he was also consuming modern jazz, especially Miles Davis and John Coltrane and the acoustic guitarists Davy Graham, Bert Jansch and John Renbourn. Nick was actually beginning to enjoy himself. In his elaborate, flowery style, he wrote home to his parents, 'It may surprise you to hear that during the last few weeks I've been extraordinarily happy with life and I haven't a clue why. It seems that Cambridge can, in fact, do rather nice things to one if one lets it. And I'm not sure that I did let it before. I think I've thrown off one or two rather useless and restrictive complexes that I picked up before coming here.'[23]

One of Nick's favourite Cambridge haunts was The Criterion, a spit-and-sawdust pub on Market Passage. Brian Wells remembers it fondly as 'the hip pub where people smoked dope'. Run by Len and Flovie Thompson, it was one of the few places in Cambridge where students and locals mingled. Among the regulars was Jenny Lacey, now a BBC executive, who would meet her school friends, including the future Pink Floyd guitarist David Gilmour, amid the tobacco tin ash trays and tar-stained walls. If you walk down Market Passage today from the market square, the site of the pub is on your right, down a set of steps next to the Qi Bar. It was at the Criterion that Nick met a young nurse and announced to Brian Wells that he'd fallen in love. Unfortunately he'd forgotten to write down her name or number and in spite of many nights spent patrolling the pubs of Cambridge he never found her again.

Cambridge was a very male environment in those days. There were only three women's colleges and no mixed colleges at all. Most of the students' sex lives were conducted with girls from the teacher-training colleges or 'the Tech' (now APU – Anglia Polytechnic University). Even so it's surprising that so few women appear in stories about Nick Drake. Here was one of the best-looking, most eligible men at Cambridge, tall, handsome, softly spoken and a guitarist to boot. But apart from Peter Rice's recollections of the girls in his room at Fitzwilliam there is little evidence that Nick was enjoying the fruits of the late 1960s sexual revolution. At a party near Selwyn College, where Brian Wells had room L22 in the modern Cripps Court, Nick claimed to have fallen in love again. 'There was nothing there for me so I left early,' recalls Brian, 'and about an hour later there was a bang on my door and it was Nick, quite drunk, and he came in and said, "Y'know I really thought I was going to fuck Gaynor tonight and she's disappeared."' Brian didn't think he was 'that upset' and he may have been covering up the fact it was he who had left early rather than the mysterious Gaynor. Either way he had to make his way back to his digs in the dead of night down the poorly lit Grange Road. 'I had this bloody great textbook of physiology,' recalls Brian Wells, 'and he said, "Can I borrow this", and he stuck a candle on it, put it on the handlebars of my bike and wobbled away drunk.'

Brian Wells had been close to Nick from the moment they met in 1967. Introduced by a mutual friend called Pete, a student at Caius who ran the Cambridge University Buddhist Society, they had a strong shared interest in music (especially some of the American artists whose albums Brian had bought during his gap-year trip to San Francisco) and getting stoned. 'He would sometimes come back from London and say, "I'm now in a position to turn you on", which meant he had a lump of black Nepalese in his pocket!' But during 1968 Brian began to notice that his friend was drifting away.

'He was aloof; he could be arrogant. I got a bit fed up with it. He had these special friends in London and was a bit mysterious about it. I know we got on and I made him laugh at times, but I wasn't part of his cool set.'

Nick's 'cool set' wasn't based around his music business associates either. With a room in his sister's flat in Battersea always available, he was spending an increasing amount of time in nearby Chelsea with a group of wealthy socialites and debutantes he'd met during his gap year. He loved to hang out with Julian Lloyd, his girlfriend Victoria Ormsby-Gore, Derek Fitzgerald, Ben Laycock and other members of London's flower-power intelligentsia, smoking dope and taking the occasional LSD trip in their elegant apartments. He would also go away with them on leisurely country weekends to Wales and the Isle of Mull. Julian Lloyd took the well-known photographs[24] of Nick on a beach during one such holiday in Harlech, home of the Ormsby-Gores. Through them Nick met the photographer Alex Henderson, whose partner at the time, Sophia Ryde, he described as 'a fair-haired and very pretty debutante with a doll-like face'. Sophia (it rhymes with higher) would become a key figure in Nick's life, perhaps the nearest thing to a girlfriend, though she prefers the description 'best (girl)friend'.

Meanwhile the team at Witchseason were getting frustrated with Nick's lack of urgency. He wasn't reachable by phone so they had to wait for him to ring or visit them before they could make arrangements to get on with recording his first album. The £10 a week stipend disappeared fast, mostly into a Cambridge or Chelsea dope dealer's pocket, and Nick was always short of money, so Brian Wells showed him how to make free calls at a public phone box by tapping the black keys on the handset cradle. Using advice printed in *Oz* magazine, Nick also learned how to phone London by dialling a long number that routed the signal through various exchanges for the price of a local call. But he was always elusive, never predictable; capable of warmth and affection, but never quite reliable enough to form a staunch friendship or be a dependable workmate. Brian Wells covered up for him in Cambridge on more than one occasion: 'I remember he left a pile of books in my room in Selwyn and I took them back to the English Faculty library saying, "Sorry these haven't been returned sooner – the person who took them out has had a nervous breakdown." It was all bullshit, but the librarian said, "I'm so sorry to hear that and of course it'll be fine." Nick thought that was very funny.'

Although Nick could be undemonstrative in company and difficult to engage in small talk, he seems to have had no difficulty playing live while he was at Cambridge. 'He loved performing,' says Joe Cobbe, who played lead guitar in 117, and spent many hours jamming with him in Nick's rooms and in his own at Trinity College. Like most guitar players of that generation, Joe still enjoys performing the 1960s folk club standard Angi,[25] written by Davy Graham and popularised by Bert Jansch and Paul Simon. 'Whenever I play it people say, "I like your version better than Jansch, better than Davy Graham", and I say, "But it's not my version, it's Nick Drake's."' Joe Cobbe's verdict on Nick's guitar technique is forthright: 'Nick was the best guitarist I ever knew, technically superb, tremendous feel, absolutely impeccable.'

His fellow Lounger Paul Wheeler, also no mean guitarist, describes Nick's finger-picking technique as 'consistent and compact', a basic clawhammer style using the thumb and forefinger of the right hand, strongly influenced by John Renbourn. In his brilliant essay on Nick for *Mojo* magazine published in 1999, Ian McDonald, now sadly himself a victim of suicide, recalled a spring day 30 years earlier in his room in King's College: 'There were a dozen or so loafers listening to the folk/jazz musicians among us when my friend Paul Wheeler put aside his guitar and introduced a fellow singer-songwriter sitting quietly beside him: "Nick." After a few moments spent checking his tuning (but perhaps to let the intervening hubbub hush), this tall, elegant person – at whom all the women in the room were now intently gazing – began to play, craned over his small-bodied Guild guitar and staring at the carpet as his long fingers moved deftly across the fretboard while he sang low in a breathy beige voice … My eyes met those of another friend, a pianist with a jazz penchant. He silent-whistled: what have we here? "Wow," chorused the gathering at the end of the song, "that was great, really nice" … Nick Drake was class. We all knew that.'

Nick appeared several times at The Bun Shop, an old pub on St Tibbs Row, which was demolished in the mid-1970s during the construction of the Lion Yard shopping complex. It's also likely that he played at informal folk nights upstairs at the Red Cow (now trendy bar brb@the cow) opposite the Cambridge Corn Exchange, where Paul Wheeler had a residency. He played with Robert Kirby at the Lady Mitchell Hall. And in the summer of 1969 Nick and Robert Kirby put another string section together to play at Brian Wells' girlfriend Marian's 21st-birthday party at the Pitt Club[26] on Jesus Lane. So Nick Drake was not the withdrawn aesthete of popular mythology. Brian Wells remembers him coming round to Selwyn College one day to borrow an amplifier and some leads from the Streaka Peach mobile disco, which Brian was running with a friend. 'He was keen to make sure everything was working. He was very hands-on, very good with electronics, like his dad.'

* * *

DURING NICK'S increasingly regular trips to London, plans for his first LP began to take shape. It was to be called *Five Leaves Left*, the message contained in packs of Rizla cigarette papers, a part of every dope smoker's kit. Joe Boyd's musical vision was similarly of its time. The music business was starting to talk about albums not singles, studios were getting more sophisticated and everyone had listened to The Beatles and Brian Wilson introducing strings, brass, choirs and all sorts of trickery into the traditional rock 'n' roll setting. One thing Joe definitely wasn't making was a 'folk' album. He loved the way The Incredible String Band were bringing different instrumentation into British acoustic music and he was impressed by the way acoustic guitarists and singer-songwriters like Leonard Cohen, Judy Collins and even Georges Brassens had embellished their records with classical instrumentation, choral arrangements and jazz textures. All this was music to Nick's ears. He felt an immediate bond with Joe Boyd, as he had done with Robert Kirby. Here was someone who not only appreciated his songs and guitar playing, but really understood the scale of his musical imagination and ambition.

Through Joe Boyd, Nick met John Wood, the other key figure in his recording career. While Joe was the producer in a Hollywood sense – he organised the sessions, booked the studios and recruited the session players – the legendary John Wood, credited as the engineer, was responsible for the sound of Nick's records. Seminal English hits from Pink Floyd's See Emily Play to Squeeze's Cool For Cats bear the imprint of John Wood. Musicians loved him and still do. Even now he is regularly sought out in the Scottish guesthouse[27] he runs with his wife Pam, and brought back to work in a recording studio by an artist or a band who want that warm, clean Woody sound. He and Nick hit it off immediately, Woody the perfectionist soundman, Nick the perfectionist musician. John Wood told

Belgian radio: 'He knew what he wanted and if he didn't get it, he would do it again, which is why it took such a long time for the first record to come out.'[28] They convened regularly at John Wood's second home, a remarkable eight-track studio called Sound Techniques, constructed by Woody and a former BBC vision mixer Geoff Frost in the old Chelsea dairy at 46a Old Church Street, SW3. Frost had designed the studio with its TV gallery-style control room up a flight of stairs, and built the mixing desk himself. John Wood made the staircase on the opposite side of the studio, which ran up to a green room and kitchen. If you visit the site today, you'll see the entrance to the old premises built in 1908 down an alley on the opposite side of the road from the offices of Warner Bros Records.

It should have been a welcoming, hospitable atmosphere, but the early sessions, fitted in between Witchseason's other projects including Fairport Convention's *Unhalfbricking* album, didn't go well. On the extracts that have emerged on bootlegs, Nick sounds tight and anxious, even starting Time Has Told Me twice. 'Oh, sorry,' he says, 'got the tempo wrong.' The stodgy version of The Thoughts Of Mary Jane recorded in December 1968 includes some of Richard Thompson's most ineffectual lead guitar playing and no flute. Decamping to Morgan Studios in early 1969, the team tried adding a flute to Three Hours, but that didn't work either. There was tension between Nick's clear vision of what the songs should sound like and the newly fashionable notion of using the studio as an instrument. Since The Beatles had pioneered the idea of writing and developing their music in the studio instead of simply recording a live performance, producers and engineers wanted to experiment with new sounds and textures. Nick was determined to reproduce the sounds he heard in his head.

There are two stories from the *Five Leaves Left* sessions, both concerning orchestral arrangements, which taken together, encapsulate the mood of the recording and the role the inexperienced but stubborn Nick Drake took in them. Knowing that Nick envisioned strings on several tracks, Joe Boyd commissioned Richard Hewson, who had recently arranged Mary Hopkin's worldwide hit Those Were The Days for Apple and would go on to score the strings for The Beatles' *Let It Be* album. Hewson didn't come cheap and it was a disappointment when the arrangements arrived and, as Joe Boyd says, 'they were much more kind of mainstream ... they didn't fit the mood of Nick's music at all'. Only then did Nick reveal that he knew a musician in Cambridge who could probably do the job. Joe Boyd was unimpressed – 'I don't want an amateur, I don't want Nick's friend from Cambridge. This is competing with Leonard Cohen'[29] – but eventually he relented and Robert Kirby was asked to submit his arrangements. A few weeks later Joe Boyd was sitting in the control room at Sound Techniques while Nick was singing Way To Blue with a live string section scored and conducted by Robert. 'Finally all the mic faders came up', Joe told BBC Radio 2, 'and John and I just looked at each other and said, "Well this is amazing, this is gorgeous." And we were absolutely stunned.'

Shortly afterwards, Nick and Robert stunned them again.

Having got used to the idea that Robert Kirby could do anything, John and Joe were astonished to hear that he didn't feel confident enough to tackle the album's melancholic masterpiece River Man. 'Robert said, "I really don't think I'm up to it",' recalls Joe Boyd: 'I know what Nick wants and I can't do it.' So the Witchseason budget was stretched again to employ the venerable Scot Harry Robinson, a celebrated orchestral composer and bandleader, who had tasted chart success as leader of Lord Rockingham's XI, the house band in Jack Good's TV series *Oh Boy*.[30] Robinson was asked to echo the drama and tension of Delius and Ravel, something he was used to after his stint as arranger on Hammer horror films like *Countess Dracula*. Joe Boyd explained how River Man came together. 'Nick sat there and played him the song and then he hummed some lines that he had in mind for a string part. Harry showed up two weeks later at the studio with the business. And we did it live, vocals, guitar, everything.'

Apart from the strings and Nick's guitar and vocals, the other defining sound of the first album is Danny Thompson's acoustic bass playing. In 1968 Thompson had become a founder member of The Pentangle with two of Nick Drake's guitar heroes, Bert Jansch and John Renbourn. Nick was flattered to have such an eminent musician playing on his album, especially as he was such a fan of Tim Buckley, who had used Danny on his recent UK tour. But unfortunately the two never actually played together. Danny only remembers overdubbing his languorous bass parts while Nick sat and smiled beatifically in the corner of the studio.

Perhaps because they were all so busy, perhaps because they were all so stoned, none of Nick's associates on the sessions seem to have picked up on the relentless despair and foreboding in his lyrics. They may even have thought he was simply affecting the melancholy style and spirit of the time and trying to ape Leonard Cohen. But while hindsight can undoubtedly lend heightened meaning to some of the songs, there is plainly a restless, disturbed quality in Nick's writing, which suggests that he was using his lyrics, consciously or subconsciously, to tell us something about himself. Time Has Told Me, superficially a melancholic love song, talked about 'a troubled mind' and leaving 'the ways that are making me be what I really don't want to be'. Place To Be, which features on the 'work tape' from 1969, contains the lines 'I'm darker than the deepest sea' and 'I'm weaker than the palest blue' and suggests that disillusionment with the music business, if not life itself, had already set in. Fruit Tree is perhaps the most remarkable example, a chilling prediction of Nick's own reputation – 'safe in ... the earth, that's when they'll know what you were really worth'.[31]

* * *

WHILE THE album was being recorded, Joe Boyd started to think about artwork. In the wake of The Beatles' *Sergeant Pepper*, this was an era when a clever gatefold sleeve could sell an album. One of the releases scheduled by Island Records for 1969 would be Jethro Tull's *Stand-Up*, with a sleeve that opened like a children's book to reveal pop-up drawings of the band. Joe knew that compelling photographs of his handsome, brooding new charge would be key to attracting listeners at a time when radio play for acoustic singer-songwriters was so limited. The photographer he turned to was Keith Morris, a member of the infamous *Oz* magazine team, who had recently been working with Nick's Witchseason stablemates The Incredible String Band.

In a glittering career, which would include famous shoots for Marc Bolan and Led Zeppelin,[32] this was Keith Morris's very first album-sleeve commission. He came to the Witchseason office on London's Charlotte Street near the Post Office Tower and then met Nick in a nearby café. He wanted the job badly, although he had serious reservations about shooting a new artist who had no experience of working with a photographer. But they clicked immediately. 'He was a likeable cove, very quiet, personable, a bit callow,' he says. 'I think the thing that struck me most was in this era of exotica he was in the black jacket. He looked like a public schoolboy on a weekend pass. No tie-dye, no fringes, no loon pants.' Keith sensed that the locations would be important. 'It was very co-operative – two people working together, thinking of situations where we would both feel comfortable.' He agreed to scout some appropriate locations and pick up Nick in a day or two for the session.

It was April 29, 1969, Budget Day in the House of Commons. To Keith's surprise Nick wore exactly the same clothes for the shoot that he'd worn at their first meeting.

And of course there was no money for wardrobe, lights or make-up. To make things worse, the Morris apartment had been burgled the previous evening so instead of his trusty Nikon, Keith had to use an unfamiliar borrowed Pentax. Details of the exact location of the first session are lost in the mists of time (and probably the dope smoke) but Keith Morris remembers it was a derelict house near Wimbledon Common, long since demolished. Because neither photographer nor subject was entirely happy, they moved to a second location, also a dilapidated property on the edge of the common. This was the house featured on the front cover of *Five Leaves Left*, with Nick staring out of an upstairs window, wearing the ubiquitous black jacket over a white striped shirt with button-down collar. Advocates of the theory that Nick was gay like to point to the fold of his blue jeans in the shot, which is said to show an erection produced by his admiration for the photographer. Others think this view is ... well, bollocks.

After shooting a few portraits on the common itself, Keith drove Nick up to Chelsea and his office and apartment in Gunter Hall Studios on Gunter Grove, not far from Sound Techniques studio. Most famous in rock history for being the base of David Bowie's management company MainMan, Gunter Hall was where *Oz* magazine was laid out by Keith Morris and the designer Martin Sharp.[33] Keith sat Nick at the old wooden table in Gunter Hall with half his face in shadow and took the portrait featured in sepia tones on the inside sleeve of the first release of the album. It's a brilliant photograph, capturing both the essence of Nick – contemplative, expressionless, thoughtful – and some fascinating detail – the elegant fingers, the long thumbnail, the shirtsleeves too short for the long arms. That historic table is now in Keith Morris's darkroom in his flat near Little Venice, London.

In the afternoon, Keith and Nick drove back across Battersea Bridge to the busy Morgan Crucible factory.[34] They had an idea that Nick's image of observer and outsider would be exemplified by a shot of him standing still against a wall while busy working people rushed past. So as Chancellor of the Exchequer Roy Jenkins was sitting down after announcing some unexpected tax rises, the factory gates opened and Keith Morris's borrowed Pentax snapped the stationary Nick and various passers-by hurrying home and ignoring him. It was a trick used by the famous Henri Cartier-Bresson, the still subject in the background clearly in focus, the moving character in the foreground blurred. This was the session that produced the running man picture used on the rear sleeve of *Five Leaves Left*. To the right-hand side of the shot, cropped by the sleeve designer, is a newspaper vendor's billboard bearing the slogan 'Evening News: Budget Day'. When the board appeared on the sleeve of the 2004 CD release *Made To Love Magic*, it was doctored to read 'many years ago', a quote from the title song of that compilation.

Keith Morris is proud of his photographs but very critical of the final sleeve design for Nick's first release. 'It's shite,' he says today. 'Working for Joe's like working for the blind. What was the point of cropping the running man and putting the derelict house shot in a livid green frame'. He blames Witchseason's in-house designer Danny Halpern, a Canadian in his mid-50s who was, in Keith Morris's words, 'a bit jazz age'.

* * *

WHILE ALL this excitement was going on in London, Nick was still struggling to sustain his role as an English student at Cambridge. It was becoming increasingly difficult to balance his two lives. His tutor Ray Kelly recalls one significant episode. 'In his second year he gave me a real tutorial twitch. He went missing for two nights.' In those days students were required to apply for an exeat, which gave them permission to stay away overnight. 'I used to give them at the drop of a hat,' says Ray Kelly, 'but I wanted to know where people were. If they wanted me to make an honest man of them *post facto* then I wasn't going to be made a monkey of.' But Nick had just disappeared. 'I was on the verge of doing what we normally did … hospitals and the police … you had to find out. So I rang the parents and they said, "He's on his way back." I've no doubt he got a rocket for it.'

Fitzwilliam's annual report on Nick to Warwickshire County Council read 'Satisfactory. His ability is not great and he lacks confidence.' Noting that his attendance was 'irregular', one of his supervisors, Claire Campbell, described him as 'very silent' and lacking 'the confidence to express what he means clearly'.

Another, L Beardsley, reported that 'he does his work, has ideas but doesn't express them fluently. He has been very quiet.'

There was one occasion where Nick's two lives coincided. In June 1969, posters appeared around Cambridge advertising the Gonville & Caius College May Ball. English blues legend John Mayall was topping the bill with his new stripped-down acoustic trio. The Liverpool Scene were there with their unique blend of poetry, rock and jazz featuring Adrian Henri and Andy Roberts. Further down the bill were Fab Cab (Marcus Bicknell and Robert Kirby's choral group), Horn, an eclectic jazz ensemble featuring Iain Cameron on flute, a novelty outfit called The North-West London Contemporary Jazz Five, Tuesday's Children, White Unicorn (whose leader John Cole went on to form The Movies) and – right at the bottom, just above his friend Paul Wheeler – 'NICK DRAKE' whose 'forthcoming LP, already hailed in the press as the record of the year, was produced by Joe Boyd (producer of The Incredible String Band and Fairport Convention). Robert Kirby arranged some of the tracks on the album and his orchestra will be accompanying Nick tonight.' Reports of this gig are sketchy and contradictory. As Paul Wheeler says, 'If you can remember it you weren't there.' But it seems unlikely that the end-of-term revellers would have engaged much with Nick's plaintive and introspective music.

This may have been the moment when Nick realised he didn't belong in Cambridge. But he delayed the inevitable decision. While Robert Kirby quit his degree course at the end of his second year and moved to London, Nick was still, as the press release for *Five Leaves Left* told everyone several months later, a student at Cambridge University. His parents must have known that he was somewhat distracted by his new life in London, but in October 1969, when he was due to start his third and final year, they had already paid his fees in the expectation that he would complete his course. Warwickshire County Council had also sent its annual grant cheque for £50 to cover his living expenses. And Fitzwilliam College had allocated him a new room in a hostel at 239 Hills Road near the new site of Addenbrooke's Hospital. Surprisingly Nick even moved in there for a couple of days while he waited for an appointment with his tutor, the redoubtable Ray Kelly.

'I can see him quite clearly now, sitting in my room,' recalls Ray Kelly, 'and telling me that he was going to devote himself to his music. My line would have been, "Look, you're within nine months of a degree", which he'd probably have got – it wouldn't have been very distinguished but he'd have got it – "now that's a cushion" – that's common sense which a young person would have difficulty in seeing because of perspective. A year seems like a long time when you're 21.'

That evening, 13 October 1969, Nick picked up a ballpoint pen and a pad of blue writing paper and dashed off a letter to his tutor. Misspelling his address as 239 Hill's Road, he acknowledged the 'good advice' he had received but confirmed that "it would be best for me…to devote myself to my musical activities." He thanked Dr Kelly for taking an interest in his case, asked to be advised of 'any complications concerning college fees' and signed off his Cambridge career with an informal 'Yours, Nick Drake.'

Eight days later Ray Kelly replied to Nick at his family home in Warwickshire: 'You know that I do not agree with your decision, but I should like to reiterate my good wishes for the future.' One of Nick's parents opened the letter and it seems highly probable that this was the first they knew of their only son's momentous decision. Certainly his father was incandescent with rage and demanded Nick's presence back home. He tried everything, including blackmail, to persuade Nick to change his mind. But after two weeks of fights and long silences, he knew the game was up. On 10 November 1969, a dispirited Rodney Drake wrote to Ray Kelly, conceding defeat.

Clearly distressed by his son's decision, Rodney acknowledged that 'music is everything to him', but bemoaned the fact that he could do nothing about this 'bad mistake', which he claimed his son would soon be greatly regretting. Nick had made it plain that the 'withdrawal of financial support' would not change his mind and that he 'must go it alone from now on.' After thanking Ray Kelly for his support and counsel, Nick's father put down his pen. There is a change in the shade of ink in the final paragraphs which suggest that they were added later and they reveal just how hard Nick's decision had hit his family. 'I suppose there is no question of his place still being vacant', wrote Rodney. 'Do forgive me asking this. It is probably trying your patience too far but you will, I am sure, understand our anxiety.

Ray Kelly's reply offered no second chance. 'The decision to withdraw had to be definite and final,' he wrote, adding 'you will know that academically he was not the strongest of candidates and I told him at the beginning of the year that he would have to make an all out effort if he was to be successful'.

So that was that. The drawbridge was pulled up and Nick Drake was a full-time musician and performer. 'I was a little worried about it,' recalls Joe Boyd, 'because we hadn't really figured out what to do with Nick as a career. But I thought, "OK, it's good he's committed."'[35] At the time, Nick must have thought his life and future reputation as an artist and songwriter were poised for take-off. In retrospect this may have been the precise moment when it all peaked. He had five years left.

2. Do You Curse Where You Come From?

4. Empire

THE LATE 1960s in Britain was a time of unprecedented social upheaval. In that age of sit-ins and freak-outs, the self-proclaimed counter-culture invented by post-war baby boomers had created what came to be called the generation gap. Perhaps for the first time in human history kids and their parents simply didn't understand one another. By challenging the colonial war in Vietnam, by demanding the legalisation of cannabis, by dropping out from traditional British lifestyles, the youth of the day were in rebellion not just against some abstract notion of straight society, but against their nearest and dearest. Sons of miners and sons of judges were both asking themselves whether it was right to follow in daddy's footsteps. Children of well-to-do families were often embarrassed, even ashamed, of their privileged backgrounds, and went to great lengths by dressing in shabby clothes or changing their accents to distance themselves from what they called 'the establishment'.

No surprise, then, that Nick Drake, an essay in calculated cool, was finding it difficult to come to terms with his ancestry and the bourgeois, conservative values of his own and other upper-middle-class families. When he sang about the 'ban on feeling free' in River Man, he may well have been thinking about his own loving but stifling family life. Like many sons of successful fathers, especially those from top-drawer English society, he came to despise the burden of expectation. He'd been brought up to believe in a set of ideals and principles that seemed to have no relevance in this modern age. He wanted to escape. In another song, Hazey Jane I, he asked, 'Do you curse where you come from?'

Nick's grandfather was Ernest Charles Drake, a distinguished surgeon who commuted to London from a grand house 23 miles or half an hour's train ride away in leafy Redhill, not far from modern-day Gatwick Airport. Rodney Shuttleworth Drake was born into this comfortable Edwardian way of life on May 5, 1908, and followed the family tradition of prep school and then public school[36] at Marlborough College. Nick's dad was a capable boy, though not academically inclined, and he left school in 1925 at the age of 17 to train as an engineer. Unfortunately the early years of his career coincided with the Great Depression. In the aftermath of the Wall Street Crash in 1929 money was tight and jobs were scarce. There was one way, however, for an ambitious British chap to make his fortune. This was the golden age of the Raj.

Since the old commercial East India Company had handed control of the Indian subcontinent to Queen Victoria's government in 1858, the Brits had ruled the territory of modern India, Pakistan, Bangladesh and Sri Lanka with that peculiar mix of arrogance, violence and charm that characterised the biggest empire the world had ever known. In 1885 the neighbouring state of Burma,[37] which ran along the north-eastern coast of the Indian Ocean between India and Thailand, was absorbed too, after King Thibaw tried to confiscate the assets of the Bombay Burmah Trading Company, an Anglo-Indian timber business.

This was the company that recruited Rodney Drake in the early 1930s. We're told that the Honourable PM Thesiger, who interviewed applicants at this time, 'took pains to ensure that they had no aspirations to early matrimony'.[38] It was a man's life 'supervising the cutting and dragging of logs by the natives', as one contemporary job advert put it, and learning the art of 'girdling', making an incision in a tree to let the sap out so that it dies over a two-year period and can then float down the river, unlike a living tree. The hours were long and the work arduous in the unforgiving heat, but the young white men who ran the company were a privileged elite, supervising a largely obedient workforce of Burmese 'wallahs' and more than 1,500 elephants. One of the great characters of this period of British imperial history was 'Elephant' Bill Williams, who would become something of a war hero in the next decade. In 1934 he attended the grand opening of the Ava Bridge, a massive British-funded construction spanning the Irrawaddy River in Burma, where he was introduced to the delightful young daughter of a senior member of the Indian Civil Service. Little Mary Lloyd, known in her family as Molly, would recount this story into her 70s. That may also have been the occasion when, for the first time, she met the dapper Rodney Drake, who had risen up the BBTC to the point where he might soon be allowed to take a wife. Rodney proposed in 1936 and as soon as Molly was 21 they were married in the majestic setting of St Mary's Cathedral in Rangoon,[39] the capital of Burma, on April 14, 1937.

In the early years of their marriage the Drakes' lifestyle would have been the envy of most couples struggling with the economic hardships of 1930s Britain. They were rich, they had status and influence in the community, and they had servants. It was the world of the after-tiffin nap and the evening chota peg,[40] of right-ho, gung-ho and a jolly good show. But as British TV viewers saw in the famous 1980s series The *Jewel In The Crown* ex-pat life could be empty and unfulfilling. The Brits were in exile, self-imposed and superficially comfortable, but exile none the less. Their houses were big and beautiful but they needed big gates to keep out the disenfranchised local people who were growing restless and demanding independence from British rule. If Nick Drake saw himself as an outsider during his lifetime, well so did his parents. Molly especially, who had been brought up in the Raj, was neither British nor Indian nor Burmese, but culturally and socially rootless.

Then in 1941 things began to get much worse. The Asian territories of the Empire had escaped the worst effects of the European war. In fact the conflict had been good for business. Demand for timber had increased and, in 1940, Rodney Drake, now second-in-command at the Rangoon office of the BBTC looked after the shipping of 81,000 tons of teak to British timber factories in India, more than twice his usual output. But on December 7, 1941, the Japanese attacked the US naval base in Hawaii, Pearl Harbor, and signalled the expansion of the Nazi war into a full-blown world war. Just a fortnight later, on December 23rd, air-raid sirens sounded on the roof of the BBTC's Strand Road headquarters in Rangoon. The Japs were on their way. On January 20, 1942, families of the company's employees, including Molly, were evacuated to Bombay.[41] Like most BBTC managers, Rodney had been enlisted into the British Army, although his main role remained within the company, but as the Japanese advanced across Burma he was part of the team of Royal Engineers that laid charges at the Ava Bridge to blow it up before the enemy could cross the strategically important Irrawaddy. Eventually, on February 20th, Rodney Drake formally shut down the BBTC sawmills and timber yards as the Japanese guns thundered on the outskirts of Rangoon. The final evacuation of the city was a bloody affair. Many Brits simply didn't make it and, sad as the Drakes must have been to leave behind their home and many of their possessions, they were relieved to meet up again safely in India.

Rodney was appointed to a management position in the BBTC's head office in Bombay with responsibility for a sawmill in nearby Poona.[42] Then, almost immediately, he was posted 800 miles north to Jhelum in what is now Pakistan, where his employers had permission to start logging in new areas to supply the British Army's insatiable demand for lorry bodies, ammunition boxes and camp equipment. It was during this renewed period of upheaval that Molly gave birth to the Drakes' first child, Gabrielle, in the city of Lahore on March 30, 1944. The Jhelum site was sent a new bandmill by the Americans as part of the Lend Lease programme and when it arrived in gigantic wooden packing cases, Rodney hit on the bright idea of using them to build a house for his family. Gabrielle, known as Gaye, spent the first few months of her life literally living in a box.

Rodney Drake didn't win any military honours in the war but, in the jargon of the day, he 'did his bit'. By 1945 the BBTC had produced 105,000 tons of sawn timber in India, a huge contribution to the allied war effort in extremely difficult circumstances. And he was given an even bigger role in the post-war reconstruction of his company. After a lengthy and arduous campaign against the Japanese in Burma, Rangoon was recaptured by the 26th Indian Division of the British Army on May 3, 1945. On June 15th Louis Mountbatten held a victory parade, but by then Rodney Drake had already been back in Rangoon for a month surveying the wartime damage to his mills, offices and transport structure, and compiling a report for the Timber Project Board on how the BBTC's property could be transferred back from Army control. He was clearly a big player in the politics of the region during this time, but post-war life was very tough. Rangoon had been badly damaged. His headquarters were wrecked, there were potholes in the streets and, making things very dangerous for an ex-pat Brit, the local Burmese, having seen one invading army driven out were not about to welcome back their former colonial rulers. There were a lot of guns on the street, many of them in the hands of groups hostile to the Brits.

It soon became clear that the popular nationalist leader Aung San[43] was intent on full independence. He had sided with the Japanese until he saw they were losing and had helped the British retake his country, but now he wanted it back. Just two months after Britain pulled out of the Indian subcontinent, Burma was given its independence, on October 17, 1947. By January 4, 1948, it was a sovereign state and the former ruling class were now aliens. In the meantime Aung San and most of his cabinet had been assassinated and the country was in the grip of a full-scale communist insurrection. Rangoon was as dangerous as any city with too many guns and not enough law. It was anarchy.

It was into this turbulent atmosphere, a world away from the traditional picture of pampered ex-pat sophistication, that Nicholas Rodney Drake was born on June 19, 1948, at the Dufferin Hospital in Rangoon, attended by the family doctor Jim Lusk. Writers chronicling his early years have speculated about why his family should have quit their comfortable colonial lifestyle to return home. But Rangoon was becoming a very nasty place indeed, certainly far from ideal for a couple trying to bring up a family. During part of 1948 Rodney Drake was in North Borneo trying to agree a deal for the BBTC to start logging there. But it was clear that the company and the Drakes had come to the end of the line. Rodney managed to negotiate a final exit deal with the new Burmese authorities ensuring that the BBTC could keep 50,000 tons of logs and saw them up free of any taxes. After that everything would be nationalised. It took until March 1952 for the final logs to be delivered and, during that time, Rodney supervised the winding-down of his company's interest in Burma and began to look around for a new opportunity in England. Everything he had worked for in his business life was lost. Sure, he had plenty of money in the bank and a healthy family, so his situation was hardly bleak, but for those former members of the ruling imperial elite returning home to look for work in an England they barely knew, the early 1950s were not a time of great optimism.

5. Far Leys

FAR LEYS House is the Graceland of the Nick Drake cult. It would be fanciful to suggest that the village of Tanworth-in-Arden, Warwickshire, might one day be known as 'Drake Country', but Shakespeare isn't the only bard attracting tourists to this beautiful corner of the English Midlands. The landlord of the Bell Inn on The Green calls them Drakeys. 'They're nice people,' says Ashley Bent, 'always polite and respectful, oddly dressed but good for business. A bit weird though.' Most summer days or anywhere near the anniversary of Nick's birth or death you can find little knots of people in the churchyard or on the pilgrimage to the end of Bates Lane where the Drakes' old family house stands rather self-righteously behind its big wooden gates. Alan Fitzpatrick, a property developer, and his family, who live there now, don't welcome 'those who stand and stare when you're gone,'[44] but elsewhere the villagers of Tanworth seem resigned to their place on the dead celebrities trail. As well as Nick, they remember world motorcycle champion Mike Hailwood, also buried in Tanworth after a premature death, and the pre-war welterweight champion Jack Hood,[45] who became landlord of the Bell in the 1950s.

It was to this area of classically English rolling hills, hedgerows and farmyards that the Drakes came at the end of Empire. Rodney, Molly, Gaye, Nicky ... and Rosie.

You can take the family out of the Empire but you can't always take the Empire out of the family. Accompanying the Drakes as they started their new life in England was their nanny and housemaid from Burma. Rosie, known to the family simply as Nanny, was a Karen (pronounced Kah-reen), a member of the predominantly Christian tribe that hails from the north of the country and is still, in the 21st century, fighting a guerrilla war against the military junta that rules Burma/Myanmar. Persecuted by the Buddhist majority, by the Japanese and by the communists, Karens lived in grinding poverty and the girls often sought domestic work with prosperous British families. But when the ex-pats started to leave in the 1940s the Karens were left to suffer abuse and maltreatment at the hands of the new authorities. The Drakes were not alone in rescuing their servant from the threat of victimisation and offering her the chance of a fresh start in England. Rosie was joined a few years later by her niece Naw Ma Naw, [46] who also worked for the Drakes in Tanworth, and her friend Easter, who took a job with Cyril and Biddy Hughes across Bates Lane in another large house, called Wayside.

Tanworth-in-Arden is a curious mixture of a typical English village and a wealthy dormitory suburb. The vicar, Tim Harmer, laughs at the description of it as part-Candleford part-Beverly Hills, but the similarities to both are immediately apparent. Travelling towards the village from the six-lane M42, just six miles away, the landscape seems to have barely changed since the Drakes moved in half a century ago. There are sheep in the fields, cattle-crossing signs, neatly trimmed hedges and plenty of farm machinery on the roads. But dominating the road are the 4x4s that belong to the wealthy families who live in the spectacular mansions that surround the village: grand properties, often with eight or ten bedrooms and sweeping gravel drives, built to accommodate the newly minted manufacturing class from nearby Birmingham in the early 20th century. The Neighbourhood Watch signs at every entrance to Tanworth leave the visitor in no doubt that there's money in these parts. With its proximity to Birmingham Airport and the M40 into London, Tanworth is rapidly becoming an ideal base for international business people, but it's retained much of its olde worlde charm because it's not on the way to anywhere else so none of the commuter rat runs passes through it.

It was this combination of rural seclusion and closeness to England's second city that brought the Drakes to the area. In common with many leading figures from old imperial businesses, Rodney Drake had returned home to look for a senior position with a British company. His background made him a natural for the Midlands engineering firms trying to find their feet after World War II, and in 1952 he joined one of the most famous names in British industry, Wolseley Engineering. Although this was the company that had built the famous Wolseley motor cars under its then works manager

Herbert Austin, the vehicle side of the business had been sold off and Wolseley was now concentrating on motor cultivators, a range of electric fencing, and its sheep-shearing machine. Within a short while Nick's dad was running the company, which then employed about 500 people and turned over £1.2 million a year. Cash flow was a problem, however, and a local solicitor, Norman Lancaster, brokered a deal for a merger with another big local name. This is how Wolseley's website takes up the story today: 'On 1 May 1958 good friends Cyril Hughes, deputy Chairman of Geo H Hughes and Rodney Drake, chairman and managing director of Wolseley Engineering agree a merger. The £1 ordinary shares are quoted at 20 shillings and sixpence.' This is the same Cyril Hughes who lived in the house opposite Far Leys and took the Karen maid Easter at the Drake's suggestion. The new company was called Wolseley-Hughes. By the time Nick was recording his last album in 1972, *Pink Moon*, it had diversified into plumbing and heating components and had annual sales of £27 million. The Hughes family moved into the grand former squire's home Aspley House on The Green in Tanworth. The Drakes stayed at Far Leys, extending and improving the property until it could legitimately be described as a mansion. Today Wolseley has a market capitalisation of more than £5 billion. Nick Drake would have been a very rich man in his middle age.

Far Leys takes its name from the arable farmland that surrounds Tanworth. Ley (pronounced lee never lay) is a local spelling of lea, meaning arable land, and shouldn't be confused with the ley lines beloved of mystics and crystal gazers. From the centre of the village, walk away from the fine 14th-century parish church of St Mary Magdalene, past the Bell Inn – recently converted into a delicatessen, wine bar and chic restaurant – and west along The Green towards the Ivy Stores, now a dog-grooming and pet supplies shop. The next turning on the left, before the vicarage, is Bates Lane. Far Leys is about a quarter of mile on the left just before the road turns sharp left and heads out into open countryside. The house itself, with its Georgian windows and rather over-stated portico above a front door guarded by two potted conifers, was built for a prosperous Midlands doctor. Rodney Drake bought it from Jim Smith, a stockbroker with Albert E Sharpe in Birmingham, who allowed a Miss Tonks to run a pre-school playgroup there before the Drakes arrived. Today, slightly hidden by trees, it's imposing and slightly institutional, with the look of a between-the-wars school or a nursing home. To the left of the main house is a covered entrance for carriages and a block containing no less than four garages. Down the lane opposite are some tennis courts, a football field and the scout hut. As Bates Lane turns away from Tanworth it runs alongside the back garden of Far Leys, which stretches a couple of hundred yards down to a stream.

It's a lazy, bucolic, timeless setting. From the rear windows you can gaze out across miles of unspoilt countryside with no other buildings to remind you that you're just a few miles from Birmingham's urban sprawl. It's a landscape for dreamers and philosophers, an environment where a young boy would grow up aware of the changing seasons, the sun and the stars, with no tall buildings or street lights to hide the sky and, perhaps most significantly, complete silence.

There is a village primary school in Tanworth, right next door to the church. These days it's highly sought after by ambitious parents who want to get their children into the Warwickshire county grammar school system, which is sometimes considered more meritocratic than the comprehensive system across the county boundary in Worcestershire. But the Drake parents had been privately educated so they took the decision to send their children through the same system and a few months after their arrival in Tanworth, in the spring of coronation year, 1953, Nick was sent to join his sister at Hurst House, a pre-prep school in nearby Henley-in-Arden, where fees were 20 guineas a term, about £6,000 a year in today's money. Today, the attractive late-Georgian building is privately owned, but you can still see it up a driveway on the right as you leave Henley on the A3400 Stratford Road. In a fascinating memoir now published on the official website of the Nick Drake estate, Nick's childhood friend Andrew Hicks remembers being part of a car pool with the Drakes and other families transporting Gaye and his own sister to Edgbaston Church of England College for Girls in Birmingham and also Nick and himself the five miles into Henley. 'We travelled in our small black Standard Eight, Molly Drake's succession of Morris Minors, and the cars of a number of other parents.

Rodney Drake's Humber Hawk … always did the run to Birmingham to the girls' school and the office. For Molly and Rodney, dull or sullen silence in the car was anathema. Partly to subdue fighting in the back, but also because performance should be a universal pleasure, stories were told and songs were sung as we travelled. After leaving [nearby] Danzey we always sang, "Shall we see the mushroom tree" to the tune of an old nursery rhyme. For the Drake family, successful performance, both music and drama, were a way of life.'

Hicks describes Hurst House as 'an easy-going school where we learned the basics of reading, writing and arithmetic. After lunch we sat or lay on blankets and had "rest" and were read a story.' But another contemporary of Nick's, John Saunders, remembers a more authoritive atmosphere and regular beatings. Nick's first teacher was a Miss Jones who had a ground-floor room at the bottom of the stairs. In subsequent years he had Miss Franey, Mrs Ince and finally a Miss Smith, who Andrew Hicks describes as a 'fire-breathing Catholic'. British prep schools in the 1950s were no place for the faint hearted and the discipline of the regime must have been a shock to the gentle and artistically inclined boy from Burma.

At weekends and during school holidays, however, Nick could escape to the wonderful Far Leys, an adventure playground for boisterous six and seven year olds. Andrew Hicks remembers playing with Nick in the garden and getting covered in mud. Another time the two of them were playing in an upstairs corridor between Nick's bedroom and the playroom. 'Our game was to rush down the corridor together, to throw ourselves on to a mat and slide along on the polished wood floor. On this occasion I fell badly, with Nick on top of me. The pain in my left leg below the knee was excruciating. One of the family's two Burmese *amahs*,[47] known as Nanny, came and carried me to the couch in the playroom. I was howling as she massaged my leg ... [it] was plastered right up to the groin and I was on crutches for six weeks. The accident was nobody's fault but the Drakes were most concerned that it had happened while in their care. Molly and Nick visited me, still prostrate in my bedroom. They brought me some presents – activity games and a Noddy book – and signed my plaster. I distinctly remember Nick saying that I had been very brave.'

Andrew Hicks also has fond memories of young Nicky Drake at village children's parties, 'always immaculately turned out in neat shorts and cotton shirts, Clarks sandals and, horror of horrors, white ankle socks. He was a delightful friend ... never aggressive or pushy, and always without malice. He was sociable, joined in all the fun and got messy like everyone. He was happy, healthy and normal. With adults his behaviour was impeccable, his goodbyes and thank yous perfectly rehearsed, always addressing Mr or Mrs Double-Barrel by name. Even unbroken, his voice had a hint of the low huskiness we hear in his singing. He was the handsome, delightful child that every parent would want their own to be.'

There's only one hint in Andrew Hicks' memoir of the darkness that would eventually overwhelm his friend. 'On thinking about it,' he writes, 'Nick was one of the very few accessible contemporaries of about my own age that my parents would have seen as an appropriate social fit. So I became used to my own companionship, went for long bike rides alone or took walks through the field with the dog. I suppose life was much the same for Nick.' Childhood in a posh family in a quiet, isolated village could indeed be a torment. The phrase 'appropriate social fit' speaks volumes about the attitude of wealthy parents who kept their kids away from their working-class contemporaries, to ensure they were uncontaminated by real life. It's hard not to feel sorry for Nick, trapped in Tanworth with his family, two servants who spoke limited English and very few friends. He was a lonely little boy, a boy in a bubble. One can see the roots of Nick's later failure to connect with people in the remoteness of those early years at Far Leys.

In recent interviews his sister Gabrielle, often known in the family as Gabriell-uh as well as Gaye, has painted a more congenial picture. Speaking on a Belgian radio programme[48] in 2004 she was at pains to portray the Drakes' family life as normal, although she gave clues that she and Nick didn't really know each other very well. 'It was a close family and I suppose it was a typically sort of brother–sister relationship, really – annoying elder sister, annoying younger brother – but I certainly loved him dearly, although he used to annoy me like that. And he was stubborn and obstinate too, but I suppose I was. You can't see it in yourself but he was always very stubborn. He absolutely knew what he wanted and he was a perfectionist. And he refused really to settle for anything that wasn't precisely what he aimed for. You know, until the clouds closed in, he was always to some degree a shy boy, retiring, but full of humour, full of irony and a very popular boy at school … He seems to have been very much liked and loved.'

Much has been made of the Drake family's love of music, sometimes to the point where they're seen as the Von Trapps of Tanworth-in-Arden. And it does seem that both listening to and making music played a major part in their time together. Gaye and Nicky would enjoy the BBC Light Programme's *Children's Favourites* on a Saturday morning, and Andrew Hicks remembers a wind-up gramophone, still something of a luxury item in the mid-1950s, in the Drakes' playroom. More remarkably the family had a reel-to-reel tape recorder in their drawing room. Some time later a room at Far Leys was designated as the Music Room and gradually filled with valve amplifiers, loudspeakers and a modern Beocord tape recorder, which Rodney used to enjoy tinkering with and which he, Molly and later Nick would use to record their own musical compositions. Tanworth residents Ray and Mary Crabtree recall being treated to informal recitals by Molly Drake at the piano and she made sure that Nick was given every opportunity to inherit her talent. 'To begin with,' she said in an interview broadcast posthumously by BBC Radio 2, 'I started teaching him the piano, which was went on to the Royal College of Music. They played 'all that stuff that was on the old Pye label,' says Simon, 'with dirty lyrics like the king bee buzzing round your hive. We thought we were quite sophisticated.' One day, according to Simon, the normally reticent Nick said, 'That looks like good fun, let's start a band.' So they recruited Mike Maclaran on bass and two guitarists, Randall Keynes (grandson of the famous economist John Maynard Keynes) and Johnny Glempser, who 'couldn't keep time' and had a penchant for 'wild solos'. To help Simon Crocker come out from behind the kit to play harmonica, a boy called Payne, whose father was one of the housemasters, was asked to sit in on drums for the occasional song. Nick Drake was on piano, alto sax and, for no other reason than 'none of us could sing', according to Simon, he was the lead singer too. Ladies and gentlemen, will you welcome … The Perfumed Gardeners.

It quickly became obvious that Nick's musicianship and quiet authority made him the leader of the band. 'It was natural,' says Simon Crocker. 'He was a good arranger with a terrific musical ear, one of those nauseating guys who can pick up your instrument and play it better than you can.' Andy Murison, who saw The Perfumed Gardeners play as a warm-up act before college film society shows in the Memorial Hall says the music was 'derivative of The Stones', but although Nick stood upfront to sing songs like Smokestack Lightning, Hoochie Coochie Man and Gonna Send You Back To Walker, he was no Mick Jagger. He 'just stood still and sang or played sax,' recalls Simon Crocker.

fairly disastrous. But we plugged on and then he went to school and had some proper lessons and it was one of the proudest days of my life when he said to me, "Oh mum, I'm glad you made me go on because it's now my favourite thing."'[49]

Following her death in 1993 a tape recording emerged of some of Molly's songs, made on the same Beocord machine Nick had employed to record his early work at Far Leys. To hear her fragile voice echoing down the decades is startling, the parallels with Nick's melody lines and clipped vocal delivery almost spooky. Gabrielle has said that Molly's songs were a big influence on Nick. 'I think at the time he would have denied this rigorously, but I think they seeped into his unconscious.'[50] And there's more than a hint of the foreboding and fatalism of Nick's material in some of Molly's lyrics. One of her songs includes the lines, 'love is all beauty but make it a duty and love will lie right down and die'. Whether that is in any sense autobiographical we can only guess. Nick's musical collaborator Robert Kirby is more circumspect, but acknowledges Molly as inspiration. 'It would be foolish to say Nick's songs sound like his mother's. They don't. His mother's songs are very between-the-wars theatre, Noël Coward, revue songs they used to be called. And they are very skilled, very beautiful songs. She had a great voice and … some of the harmonies, some of the melodic lines, and the way the harmonies fit against them … you can see where Nick came from.'[51] Rumours have circulated for some years that the Nick Drake estate may release some of these recordings on a forthcoming album of Nick-related material called *Family Tree*, but apart from a tiny snatch of one song played on a cassette machine in both the Nick Drake film documentaries[52] nothing has emerged into the public domain yet.

As well as singing in the parish church choir with his sister, Nick was beginning to write songs too. Gabrielle told Patrick Humphries about an early composition called Cowboy Small and a song about celery and tomatoes. Perhaps because it liberated his imagination, perhaps because it was simply what the family did, Nick had become absorbed in music. 'He was always interested in music,' said Molly. 'Nick as a little tiny child aged about one would get up and be conducting away. Every time any music started on Nick would stand and conduct, and we always used to say he's going to be a famous conductor. Really from then on it was music the whole time. It was just the main part of his life I think.'[53]

6. Marlborough

OUTSIDE wealthy English society it would seem an act of unimaginable cruelty to send a shy eight-year-old child away from home to boarding school. But for families like the Drakes it was the norm and often still is. Education in one of the great public schools of England is a much sought-after prize, supposed to guarantee that your children speak with the right accent, meet the right people and are properly equipped to 'get on' in the armed forces, the law, the Church or the City. To ensure access to one of these institutions at the age of 13, children need to attend a preparatory school, which gets them ready, both academically and socially, for the Common Entrance exam and the passport to continued privilege. Gaye was already attending the genteel Wycombe Abbey School for Girls in Buckinghamshire and, in 1957, a few weeks before his ninth birthday, the Drakes' only son was packed off to Eagle House School in Berkshire, some 120 miles from Tanworth-in-Arden.

Eagle House is now a mixed school, but in those days it was for boys only. Owned by next-door Wellington College, a top public school with a tradition of sending well-rounded chaps to nearby Sandhurst for officer training and a career in the British Army, it occupies a grand Victorian mock-Tudor building sitting in about 30 acres of woodland in between the M3 and the M4 to the west of London. In the 1950s, before the motorways were built, most of its customers would probably have described it as 'near Ascot'. The headmaster of the day was Paul Wootton, an austere classicist whose image was softened by a glamorous younger wife, but who set great store by discipline alongside the inculcation of what teachers of the day called the 'three Rs' – reading, (w)riting, and 'rithmetic.

It's difficult to tell how easily Nick coped with this shock to his young system. But like most children he found a way to adapt to the challenges and privations of living away from his family and fitting in with a new crowd. Indeed by the end of his four years at Eagle House he was awarded the title of Head Boy, so he must have prospered in that regimented, claustrophobic atmosphere. Supporters of the boarding school concept always stress how often young boys (and it is still mostly boys) quickly get over the shock of missing mummy and start to enjoy the pleasures of a permanent summer camp. Critics counter that this is simply because they've become institutionalised and will find it difficult to cope with the real world. But it's surely no accident that so many boarding school-educated men find themselves in the legal profession or the military or the civil service or somewhere else where the old rules still apply.

We can get a clue about the survival strategy young Master Drake designed for himself from the testimony of another

Nick who overlapped at Eagle House for a year and who would later play a significant role in his posthumous career. As Head of A&R[54] at Island Records in the 1980s, Nick Stewart commissioned the *Heaven In A Wild Flower* album, the first compilation of Nick Drake's work. Back in 1960/61 he was the young boy whose peg was next to Nick Drake's. The numbers alternated across a corridor: Drake NR was 36, Stewart NJS was 38.

Nick Stewart remembers his namesake as 'tall, handsome, athletic and upright'. Photographs of the time show him in the Eagle House uniform of blazer and flannels or grey suit with short trousers, red tie, long grey socks and a bright red cap bearing the school motto *sublimiora petamus* (let us seek higher things). Perhaps because of their age difference the younger Nick found the senior one 'rather supercilious, rather aloof, looking down on us younger kids'. This was the pre-Beatles rock 'n' roll era and a couple of Nick Stewart's contemporaries were big Elvis Presley fans. One parents' day, their mums turned up with Elvis albums as presents and shortly afterwards a poster of the King was found on the wall of one of the dormitories. For headmaster Paul Wootton, who believed that pop music was a pernicious influence on his young charges, this was a very serious matter. At morning assembly the offending poster was produced and the perpetrators of the heinous crime of enjoying the devil's music were named and shamed. 'Nick Drake looked down his nose at us for being silly little boys', says Nick Stewart. 'There was no sign of rebellion. I would have expected him to become a lawyer or a member of the Foreign Office, something very conventional.'

Nick did music lessons and was a member of the chapel choir, but in spite of Molly Drake's enthusiastic descriptions of her son's early love of music, there's no evidence that he was especially keen on it at Eagle House. He may, however, have been influenced by one of his French teachers, a Mr JR Watson, who had a very unlikely claim to fame. Fellow academics knew him as the author of the celebrated French primer *La Langue Des Français*, still in print today, but the boys were more interested in the fact that he had written the lyrics for the UK's entry in the 1960 Eurovision Song Contest, a ditty called Looking High High High, sung by Bryan Johnson, brother of Teddy, who was half of a chart-topping duo of the day with Pearl Carr.

Perhaps the best clue to Nick's developing personality was given in his final report from Eagle House. His father Rodney recalled that the headmaster had written 'nobody knows him very well'.[55]

At the age of 13, Nick Drake passed his Common Entrance exam and in December 1961 bade goodbye to his friends at Eagle House. After Christmas he packed his trunk into the boot of Rodney's luxurious black Humber and headed not for Wellington College, but south to Wiltshire and his father's old Alma Mater Marlborough College. Another all-male institution, Marlborough (always pronounced Morl-bruh, never Marl-bruh) was run along classic public school lines. Readers of the famous Billy Bunter or Molesworth books

Nick with photographer Keith Morris's Hasselblad in the garden of 112 Haverstock Hill, London, June 1970. Note the short sleeves on one of his father's old shirts.

REX FEATURES

LARRY AYRES

Rodney and Molly Drake in 1982.

The actress Gabrielle Drake, Nick's older sister.

Far Leys House, Tanworth-in-Arden, the 'Graceland' of the Nick Drake cult.

Saxophonist Drake NR (2nd row from the left, 2nd from back) in the Combined Cadet Force band, Marlborough College, 1965.

Drake NR (2nd row from rear, 4th from right) at Eagle House Preparatory School, probably 1960. His friend Nick Stewart is in the front row, 4th from left.

Freshman Nicholas Drake (2nd row from rear, 5th from right) in his first week at Fitzwilliam College Cambridge University, October 1967.

School friends Jeremy Mason (left) and Nick at Victoria Station London en route to college in Aix-en-Provence, July 1967. After his summer of love (and drugs) in the south of France and then Morocco, Nick would never be the same again.

The Gate of Humility at Gonville and Caius College Cambridge where Nick and the Loungers met to *obſerve how ſtrange creatures ye Lord hath made.*

The austere modernist lines of Fitzwilliam College Cambridge. This was the main entrance in Nick's time.

Nick's friend and string arranger Robert Kirby (far left) with his choral group the Gentle Power of Song, November 1967. The beard came later. Marcus Bicknell, the great networker, stands at the back.

Nick's manager and producer Joe Boyd, looking uncannily like Nick himself, introducing an Incredible String Band show at the Royal Festival Hall London, probably March 1968.

An unused shot from the first Keith Morris session, Morgan Crucible Factory, Battersea, London, April 29th 1969. The 'running man' shot from the same session became the rear sleeve of Nick's first album *Five Leaves Left*.

would instantly recognise the world that Nick Drake was entering: a world of petty rules, canings, prefects, bullying, tuck shops and postal orders from home. The Victorian practice of fagging, where the youngest pupils were forced to act as servants to senior boys, had been abolished by this time, but, as one of Nick's friends Simon Crocker remembers, 'there were still plenty of silly rules about how many buttons you had to have done up on your blazer'.

Marlborough did at least have the advantage of being slightly nearer home than Eagle House (about 90 miles instead of 120), but as Nick now knew very few, if any, children of his own age in Tanworth, this would have meant little to him. He could be sure, however, that he was one of the chosen people. Marlborough had been established in the 19th century as a school for the sons of clergy and although it now fished for pupils in a wider pool, it would have left no doubt in the minds of its new boys that they had 'arrived'. If Nick Drake sometimes seemed aloof or superior to people he met in later life, we can attribute his demeanour to the simple fact that he spent such a long time in a school environment, as well as a family, that encouraged children to believe they really were superior.

The College sits in the middle of the ancient town of Marlborough on both sides of the A4, then the main road from London to the West Country. It's quieter now, since the M4 motorway was built to the north of the town, and you can get a sense of the atmosphere of the College without risking life and limb dodging the traffic. Rather like Cambridge, students live in small communities dotted around the campus. In his first year Nick lived in Barton Hill, one of the so-called Out Houses, which you can see if you walk or drive westwards along the A4 today. After you pass the College entrance and its cathedral-style Victorian gothic chapel, Barton Hill is the third building on your right. In 1962, for his second year (known in Marlborough as the Remove), Nick moved across the road and into one of the College's finest buildings, a mansion built for the Duke of Somerset in the early 1700s. C1 House, situated on the main courtyard of the College, which is known simply as Court,[56] had also been a coaching inn called The Castle and later became the first home of Marlborough College. It was in C1 that Drake NR came under the influence of the formidable Dennis Silk, his housemaster.

Still a sprightly man in his 70s, Dennis Silk is another key figure in Nick's story. Settling into a plump leather chair in his London gentlemen's club, he remembers him well. 'He was a very private person and it seemed to me there were great depths there, which I never completely plumbed although I was very fond of him. He was a dreamy boy, very "Wake up, Drake! Oh sorry sir!" But I liked him. I liked his whole family. His mother and father were ideal parents from a housemaster's point of view. Molly was delightful and very pretty and his lovely sister Gabrielle was equally nice. I was glad to have Nick in my house.' Simon Crocker, who met Nick when they were both in Barton Hill, but later moved to Littlefield, one of the Out Houses, says the same. 'His mum was very pretty. Dad was much older and wasn't that well. They were really decent, really nice people, I liked them a lot.' Andy Murison shared a study with Nick and Martin Scott, and remembers going to parties at Far Leys: 'doting mother, very good-looking, very elegant, Nick was the apple of the eye. Nothing was too good for him.' He had a precise, considered air about him. Contemporaries recall a confident, slightly unapproachable, almost aristocratic bearing, 'quietly authoritative' according to Simon Crocker. The image was reinforced by a cut-glass accent. 'His pronunciation was very exact,' says Andy Murison, 'and he was very articulate.'

Nick's early passion at Marlborough was sport. It has been well documented that he was a fast runner and held a record for the 100 yards' dash, which stood for many years. Simon Crocker thinks the appeal of athletics for Nick was that it was a solo activity: 'He could do it on his own; he didn't have to put up with other people's shortcomings.' Nick did play team games but never with much enthusiasm. 'He had tremendous potential as an athlete; he ran like the wind,' says Dennis Silk, 'but rugby football was certainly not his *métier* although he did very well at that too, simply because no one could catch him.' His housemaster blamed 'poorish eyesight' for Nick's comparative lack of success at ball games and Simon Crocker remembers him wearing glasses though 'not all the time, just for reading'. Mostly 'he'd kind of scrunch his eyes up'.

Academically, Nick's public school career was mixed. In his early years he was considered good enough to be put into classes with older boys – accelerated, as teachers describe it. Andy Murison is almost exactly the same age as Nick, but was an academic year behind him. At the time he thought this was because Nick was clever, but now believes that he may have been 'over-stretched'. The statistics support this interpretation. Although Nick successfully got through two GCE O-levels[57] (French and Latin) a year early, he passed just five more (English Language, English Literature, German, Maths and History) and failed a subject called Physics with Chemistry in 1963. Typically, a high-achieving public school pupil would achieve nine or ten passes at this level so a score of seven suggests that Nick's mind was on other things. His own description of his record at Marlborough, written on his UCCA form[58] on September 18, 1966, gives us a clue to how his interests and ambitions had begun to change. 'Member of various musical societies, have played in school orchestra, concert band, dance band etc. Also interested in art, Goya and modern art in particular. School athletics colour,[59] played in hockey XXII[60] and rugger XV.' Music had become his first priority. 'Nick was an extraordinary boy,' says Dennis Silk, 'because in a school where games were rather over-worshipped, he didn't like missing music lessons for rugger.'

By 1964/65, when Nick should have been studying hard for his A-levels, the exams that would get him a place at university, he was playing music of one sort or another every day. Not the guitar, though – that passion was yet to develop. 'Nick could play the first movement of Grieg's piano concerto,' says his roommate Andy Murison, 'and that was very impressive.' He could play the clarinet well too and knew the

popular hit Stranger On The Shore note for note. Simon
Crocker played with Nick in the College's military band. 'We
had to do CCF[61] so we chose something that was just fun. Nick
played sax, which he was moving into from the clarinet and I
played drums. We played Supremes numbers and other cool
things as well as the military stuff. It was absurd all that
marching. On Field Day some old general came to inspect us
and Nick and I just watched all the boys in their uniforms
fainting. It was hilarious.'

One thing the boys never lacked at boarding school was
time. If you weren't the games-playing type there were three
afternoons a week as well as endless hours in the evenings and
even in the early mornings before classes started, which could
be devoted to music. Nick was fortunate that the master of
Marlborough at the time was John Dancy, a renowned biblical
scholar, who had a more enlightened view of scholastic attainment
than some of his predecessors. He encouraged the performing
arts, including music, as much as academic study and sport, and
gave the boys room to develop their own artistic and creative
pursuits. No surprise then that in the immediate wake of The
Beatles and The Stones, beat groups started springing up all over
Marlborough College. Dennis Silk talks wistfully about how the
traditional college dances with a local girls' school were suddenly
invaded by 'this loud electronic music'.

As well The Four Squares and Les Blues En Noir, there
was Sex Love & Society Plus One, which occasionally
featured Nick's friend Simon Crocker on drums (using his
older brother's kit), and a pianist called Peter Malcolm, who

'There was no performance as such.' One of Nick's best friends, Jeremy Mason, has fond memories of Nick sitting at a grand piano and performing a breathtaking version of Mose Allison's laconic 12-bar blues Parchman Farm. 'It was wonderful; partly because he had a cold, partly because he'd had a couple of beers.' 'He loved performing,' says Simon Crocker, 'and it always astonished me when I heard later that he found it difficult. He certainly didn't lack confidence at Marlborough.'

In a letter to his parents Nick confirmed the importance of music in his school life. 'My musical activities seem to be in full swing already. There was a film show on Saturday and nobody seemed prepared to provide music before it so I formed a small group and after one practice we went on and attempted to play ... In one number I completely forgot the words of the last verse and we ground to an embarrassing halt ... However the most amazing thing was quite a lot of people congratulated us afterwards and said they had thoroughly enjoyed it. The fact that 90% of all Marlburians are musical ignorami is certainly helpful at times.'[62]

The teenage Nick Drake that emerges from the recollections of his contemporaries at school shows little sign of the social difficulties he was to experience only a few years later. He was shy, reticent, not the life and soul of any party, but apparently charming, dryly amusing and well liked by everyone. 'I don't think I ever saw Nick lose his temper,' says Simon Crocker. 'I mean, he would go quiet on people but that was it.' He had lost some of the superciliousness and pomposity he demonstrated at Eagle House and, while no rebel, was less prepared to go along with authority. His housemaster Dennis Silk made him a house captain, one of five or six monitors, or prefects, for the 50 boys of C1, but not head of house, because 'that would have meant he would have had to take a very positive disciplinary line, which he wouldn't have enjoyed'.

Nick was never one of the bad boys at Marlborough, but he enjoyed the company of some of the more eccentric and less mainstream members of the school. He formed a strong bond with Jeremy Mason of B2 House, who was probably not the kind of boy of whom the Drake family would have approved. 'He thought he was cool but he was just thick,' says Andy Murison, 'though we all liked him because he was great fun.' 'Yes, I was in a dense persons' stream,' says Jeremy today, 'but only because I couldn't see any point in working for the exams.' Nick and Jeremy indulged their shared passion for French Gauloises cigarettes on long walks by a disused railway line and through a tunnel near the school. 'We used to have deep discussions about Balzac or Camus or Jean-Paul Sartre, and about jazz, Coltrane, Miles Davis. We actually did all that stuff – that's what one did,' says Jeremy. 'Can you imagine teenagers today being serious about that kind of stuff?'

Jeremy's descriptions of those carefree years evoke an era that is hard for more cynical generations to imagine. It was a uniquely untroubled time to be young. The war and the Empire had gone and the regimentation of English society was breaking up. But the constraints of the 1970s, unemployment, social unrest, economic depression, hadn't yet arrived. So for a brief window, young people were freer than ever not only to think about, but to actually do almost anything they liked.

* * *

NICK AND his close friends in the privileged world of Marlborough seem never to have given a thought to such prosaic matters as passing an exam or getting a job. They simply assumed that with their connections, they would do all right. 'Casual was what you were meant to be,' says Jeremy Mason, 'that was the coolest thing of all. "Laid back" as we'd say now. You had to walk as if nothing mattered, talk as if nothing mattered and for many of us it didn't.'

It is hardly surprising, then, to see Nick Drake's A-level results. When the envelope landed on the doormat of Far Leys in the summer of 1965, he would have been expecting to pass all three of the subjects he'd taken at grade C or above. He probably hoped for a couple of As or Bs to smooth his path to university. Instead, the paper from the Oxford & Cambridge Joint Board read, 'History (D), English (E), Latin Translation with Roman History (Fail)'. After 12 expensive years of private education this was not the return on investment for which Rodney Drake had been looking.

What made this academic failure all the more embarrassing was that Nick had already been in contact with Cambridge, clearly assuming that he would pass his A-levels with good grades. In the Fitzwilliam College archives is a hand-written letter dated April 3, 1965 to Norman Walters, then tutor for admissions, signed 'yours sincerely Nicholas Drake'. In it the sixteen-year-old Nick describes himself as 'anxious' to try for admission to Fitzwilliam and asks for the relevant application forms. He 'would very much like to come up' in October 1966 to read history.

In the summer holiday of 1965 Nick passed his driving test, a great liberation for a teenager stranded in the English countryside during vacations, and began to borrow his mother Molly's car to visit his friend from Marlborough David Wright, who lived in nearby Wolverhampton. For a while Nick and David became close friends. To Nick's parents' dismay they set off one day to hitchhike around Europe and made it to Paris, then down to Avignon and along the Côte d'Azur before the money ran out and they had to be back for school. This was a key time in Nick's musical development because David Wright was a big influence on his friend picking up a guitar for the first time. He told Patrick Humphries that he had shown Nick how to play his first chords: C, A minor, F and G7. Like so many other teenagers in the 1960s, Nick was soon captivated by the instrument.

In the autumn of 1965 Nick went back to Marlborough to work on his A-levels again. His housemaster Dennis Silk was pleased to see him. 'We thought we should have done better by him than we did. It was up to us to get it out of him.' After much discussion, it was decided that Nick should re-take Latin, drop History and study both English and British Constitution in one year instead of the normal two. It would have been a big task for someone who worked hard. Fortunately for Nick, though perhaps unfortunately for his studies, two of his best friends, Simon Crocker and Jeremy Mason, had been in the year below him so they were still at Marlborough when he returned. Nick slipped straight back into the bohemian fringe of the school. He was caned for smoking by Dennis Silk, who promises that he didn't use the old adage 'this hurts me more than it hurts you', but was clearly disappointed that a boy for whom he had such high hopes was wasting his time in village pubs and listening to music after lights-out at 11pm.

Building on their experiences in France, Nick and David Wright became experts at hitchhiking to London when they should have been asleep in their study rooms. They managed to see the celebrated organist Georgie Fame at the Flamingo Club. They saw Zoot Money & His Big Roll Band and Chris Farlowe, and they were in the Marquee Club in Soho when The Spencer Davis Group announced that they had reached number one with Keep On Runnin'. The bass player with Spencer Davis, Steve Winwood's brother Muff, who later became head of A&R at Island Records, would have been blissfully unaware that the tall, elegant sixth former at the back of the Marquee that night would one day cause him so many problems.

Nick's particular favourite band at this time was The Graham Bond Organisation, whose album, *The Sound of 65*,[63] was constantly playing while he worked in his room. He and Jeremy Mason managed to get out of Marlborough one night in October of that year to see the GBO live at the Manor House Hotel in London just north of Finsbury Park. It's one of many coincidences that fuels the Nick Drake myth that Graham Bond himself committed suicide just seven months before Nick's own tragic demise in 1974. Graham Bond is almost forgotten today, but many of the members of his band became luminaries of the British rock scene. John McLaughlin was talked of alongside Eric Clapton and Jimi Hendrix when he recorded with The Mahavishnu Orchestra in the 1970s. Saxophonist Dick Heckstall-Smith was a distinguished member of John Mayall's band. And, more impressively, bassist Jack Bruce and drummer Peter 'Ginger' Baker went on to form Cream with Eric Clapton. The GBO's *Sound of 65* is one of the records that gives us a clue about how Nick Drake's musical tastes were developing.

He liked Dylan and Donovan because he could pick out their chords and melodies on his new acoustic guitar, and he admired good lyrics. But jazz and blues were where it was really at for the cool guys at Marlborough. In February 1966, Jeremy Mason and Nick ducked out of Marlborough for another unauthorised trip to London. In a record store on Maddox Street they bought The Graham Bond Organisation's new single St James Infirmary. 'Nick's main interest was sax,' says Jeremy. 'I didn't know he played guitar at all until after we left school.' Miles Davis's *Kind Of Blue* was another big influence. The modal structure of Davis's compositions captivated Nick and showed him new ways to break free from the formulae of traditional jazz, blues and pop structures. One day Nick Drake would fuse the sensibility of jazz with the technique of acoustic folk to create his own unique form of musical expression.

* * *

DURING THIS final year at Marlborough, Nick's image hardened. He was one of the most senior boys there now and he had very clear ideas about how he wanted to portray himself. To a more conservative student like his roommate Andy Murison, Nick was 'charismatic, a cool observer of the world more than a participant in it, very together'. In a posting on one of the many 21st-century Drake websites CG Reynolds paints an evocative picture of the house captain who was now just a couple of years away from writing and performing some of the finest English music of any age. Reynolds recalls a school open day fair when 'Nick donned a denim jacket and jeans, and lounged against the pillars at the entrance of the grandest school building, C House, playing the harmonica slung around his neck, and singing Dylan, Guthrie and some early Donovan songs. This was mildly scandalising to a fairly conventionally minded boy like me – I was 20 feet away filling balloons … with hydrogen, and attaching labels to them for charity.'[64] Other pupils saw more anxiety in Nick's demeanour. Andy Murison remembers him quite assiduously doing his prep, or private study, 'in that very careful forward slopey writing. He was diligent, hard-working, he didn't cut corners.' Perhaps like many rebellious teenagers he was caught between the ambition to quit school and fear of the consequences of failure. Andy Murison's verdict is quite telling: 'Perhaps he was unsure of what he was and couldn't relax into himself.'

As England prepared to host the 1966 football World Cup, Nick sat down to re-take his A-levels. This time there could be no second chance. If he was going to live up to his parents' expectations he had to pass all three subjects well. So the results – a respectable B in English, but an E in British Constitution and another E in Latin Translation with Roman History – must have been a bitter blow. 'Rodney would have wanted more than Nick produced,' says Dennis Silk. 'He'd have been disappointed that Nick, with all his sporting and academic potential, wasn't interested in any of it really.'

Nick returned from another summer holiday in France – this time at Jeremy Mason's parents' home near Avignon – with no clear idea of what to do. His exam results weren't good enough to guarantee a place at Cambridge but his family didn't want him to submit to the ignominy of clearing, the system by which people with disappointing results could be found a place at their second, third, fourth or even fifth choice university.[65] Nick had one last option. The Oxford and Cambridge system in those days required applicants to stay on at school for a further term and take special Oxbridge-only scholarship exams known as 'schols'. If Nick could do well in those he might still get in to read English, especially with the benefit of a glowing reference from Dennis Silk imploring his old friend Norman Walters at Fitzwilliam to give young Drake a chance. One thing Nick wouldn't do, though, was return to Marlborough. He had already stayed a year longer than his contemporaries and he was anxious to escape from the school atmosphere so, as he wrote to Norman Walters on October 4, 1966, 'I am now going ahead and presuming that it will be alright to take [the exam] at Bantock's Tutorial School.' This was a cramming college known formally as the Birmingham Tutorial School, based on Harborne Road near Five Ways. Its principal, Raymond Bantock, also wrote to Fitzwilliam College asking if 'Jonathan Drake [sic] of Far Leys, Bates Lane, Tanworth-in-Arden' might be permitted to 'take the examination here'. Nick had hardly made a big impact on him.

Dennis Silk's reference for Nick, written on October 6, 1966 for his university application form, is a fascinating and prescient document:

> *Nicholas Drake is a boy who has taken a long time to mature academically. His IQ, measured when he first came to the school, was high enough to make us hope for a much more dynamic approach than he showed for several years. One always felt that there were possibilities here and yet he seemed incapable of producing. Suddenly, in his last year, after one rather poor set of results at A level he began to go forward fast and the mirror of this is the B he obtained in English this year where he had only managed an E the year before. He has left Marlborough with 4 A levels, in History, English, Latin Translation with Roman History, and British Constitution, and only in the English did he really come alive and begin to sparkle. Undoubtedly one of the things which held him back for so long was his lack of interest in History and Latin, and the freedom*

he felt when he turned over to an English course at the very end was a real emancipation which bodes well for his future. He is essentially a rather dreamy, artistic type of boy, very quiet, verging almost to the side of shyness. He loves English and this last year had a timetable especially prepared for him, by which he was able to spend a lot of time reading by himself. His whole written fluency developed enormously and people who had written him off were forced to eat their words. I strongly feel that given the chance to read English at the university he would be a very good candidate indeed. He has always had a feel for the theatre and comes from an acting family: his sister is a very successful young actress. He himself loves music and plays several wind instruments and would, I think, secretly like to be good enough to make his living in music.

He was someone who everybody liked enormously here, despite his reticence and the difficulty of getting to know him well. He was a sound House Captain and a most talented athlete who was never really deeply interested in breaking records which were well within his grasp. He is probably one of the best sprinters we have had at Marlborough since the war and yet he would much more often than not be found reading when he should have been training. He was a successful Rugby wing three-quarter but because of poorish eyesight didn't play other ball games. In conclusion I would say that he is a genuine late developer who is only now growing into his academic potential. For a long time we have despaired of him but now I genuinely feel that given a chance to read English at the university he would prove a great success and in more spheres than the purely academic one. He could give a lot to the community as well as getting a lot. He is a most delightful person to deal with.

7. Aix

ON DECEMBER 12, 1966, Norman Walters wrote to Nick with the news that his cramming had been successful. He would be offered a place, not a scholarship or an exhibition, but at least a place at Fitzwilliam College to read English, commencing in October 1967. Unfortunately Nick was not at Far Leys to read the letter. Indeed the Drakes weren't quite sure where he was so Rodney opened the envelope and responded on his behalf: 'to avoid delay I am replying to your letter offering ... a place which we accept'.[66] However, there was a catch. Norman Walters added that 'in view of the requirement in the English Tripos to translate from French into English, I should be grateful if you would let me know what arrangements you will be able to make to deal with this side of your work before coming up.' Rodney replied firmly: 'he will be spending six months from the beginning of February 1967 at the Université de Aix-en-Provence'. It was another massive investment in Nick's education by the Drake family. In 2005, the equivalent course with lodging and food costs more than 10,000 US dollars.

But it's unlikely that Nick cared. As far as he was concerned, he was about to embark on a fully funded jolly with his mates. Fellow Perfumed Gardener Simon Crocker was signed up for the course too, as was the rascally reprobate Jeremy Mason, whose family had a house nearby. The sun, the wine, the music, the girls … it sounded like heaven for a bunch of posh English refugees fleeing from the austerity of mid-1960s England and the constraints of their public school education. But it was to have far-reaching consequences. 'Without the Marlborough system we had too much freedom too soon,' says Jeremy Mason. 'For some reason this badly organised, ramshackle slightly louche life in Aix changed things for all of us. The change in everything happened in Aix.'

Aix-en-Provence, usually known simply as 'X', is a picturesque old town of pavement cafés, bookshops and exotic fountains a few miles north of Marseilles. Not unlike Cambridge, it was sidestepped by the Industrial Revolution and in 1967 it was very sleepy and slightly run-down, known mainly for its university, which specialised in French language courses for foreign students. According to Simon Crocker, 'Jeremy, Nick and I were put on a train at Victoria and told not to come back for six months. It was a real adventure.' In 1967, long before student credit cards and cash machines, booze cruises and budget airlines, the UK was not yet a member of the Common Market, or the EU as it became, and France was most definitely a foreign country. Nowadays many students take a gap year in between school and university, but in the 1960s it was quite rare. Simon believes that their parents may have seen the trip as a 1960s version of the Grand Tour, encouraging their offspring to take in some European culture.

Perhaps they hoped that the experience would take the place of National Service and help to toughen up their pampered offspring. And it was also handy that by registering a child at a foreign university, wealthy parents could avoid the £50 limit on exporting sterling which was in force during the Wilson Government's desperate (and doomed) attempt to avoid the devaluation of the pound.

The boys had made no accommodation arrangements and there were some chaotic days ahead of them when they arrived at Aix-en-Provence railway station on the Avenue Victor Hugo. Following his previous vacations, Nick spoke better French than the other two, but they struggled to find out where to enrol for their course and where to look for somewhere to stay. After a couple of nights in cheap hotels, they found two apartments in the Residence Sextius, about five minutes from the central Cours Mirabeau on Boulevard Victor Coq. There was no definite plan about how sleeping accommodation was shared. 'It was decided on the basis of who had guests or who'd picked up a girl and wanted some privacy,' says Jeremy Mason.

From the outset the three young Englishmen, free from both parental and school control, showed no inclination to work. Neither did the French university seem to care as long as it got its fees. 'As I wrote to my parents at the time, they weren't very interested in whether we turned up or not,' recalls Jeremy Mason. 'We didn't do any work at all. I think we borrowed some notes to copy them once or twice, but we didn't bother with lectures. They were in French anyway so

I couldn't understand them.' Apparently Nick liked the sound of the language and used to enjoy sprinkling his conversation with a few words when he could. Jeremy Mason remembers that after telling Nick about a particularly harrowing hitchhiking adventure, in which he had feared for his life, Nick reported the event in a letter home using the phrase 'c'est malheureux que', literally 'it's a pity, that'. 'Shows his downbeat sense of humour,' says Jeremy rather ruefully 40 years later.

There was plenty of time for music and the arts. Aix is a city of culture, proud of being the birthplace of Cézanne in 1839 and where his great friend Zola was brought up. It's a stimulating environment full of galleries, choirs, theatre groups and jazz clubs. Jeremy Mason recalls going to a bookshop with Nick and buying a copy each of Baudelaire's poems *Les Fleurs Du Mal* (Flowers of Evil). They read Dostoyevsky and Rimbaud. And they had a cheap old gramophone for which Nick bought a copy of Bach's Brandenburg Concertos, a work he was always keen to have around and which may have been the last piece of music he heard before he died just seven years later.

Those long lecture-free days were tailor-made for Nick to practise his guitar. That's what people remember about him during those months leading up to what became known as the Summer of Love. 'I never saw Nick write a song, but I did hear him tuning, tightening and slackening off strings through the night, endlessly,' recalls Jeremy Mason. 'He played interminably; it was part of the pleasure of having him around.' But was he already good enough to make it as a musician? 'One neither knew nor cared,' says Jeremy. One weekend at the Mason family house Nick recorded a few songs on a primitive cassette tape recorder. Simon Crocker 'didn't think it was fantastic. We just thought, "Well done Nick."'

One of the biggest influences on Nick's musical development at this time was Donovan. The UK music press had always been grudging in its praise for the young Scottish minstrel who seemed to be aping Bob Dylan. The superficial similarities of Catch The Wind and Blowing In The Wind hadn't helped, nor did his self-conscious appearance in DA Pennebaker's documentary film *Don't Look Back*. And when he dropped the protest-singer image and started to make pop singles like Sunshine Superman and Mellow Yellow he was declared irredeemably uncool. But in France it was different. There, the newly hippified Donovan was hailed as a major star and his presence was unavoidable on café jukeboxes. Simon Crocker bought Nick a copy of the *Mellow Yellow* album when it was released in February 1967 to play on their Philips battery record player, and Nick practised day and night to work out Donovan's tunings and chord shapes. Listening to the album today, the link to Nick's first recordings is startling. The acoustic guitar intros to Hampstead Incident and Sand And Foam could be from early Drake compositions. So could phrases like 'be that as it may' from Young Girl Blues and 'I ponder the moon in a silver spoon' from Writer In The Sun. Elsewhere there are Robert Kirby-style arrangements by John Cameron, flute passages, a double bass, conga drums, many of the sounds that Nick would use on his first album. Forget the hippy-dippy singalong title track, arranged by future Led Zeppelin bassist John Paul Jones and augmented by Paul McCartney's vocals, *Mellow Yellow* is a record that the future author of At The Chime Of City Clock knew well and loved.

Nick had enough confidence in his newly honed ability on the guitar to start gigging. He wrote to his parents: 'I'm looking round for an opportunity to start playing my guitar in public. There have in fact been one or two dances already but I've been rather lazy about it ... I went to a jazz club in Aix the other night and stood in for about half an hour with some other students. I mostly played piano, but also had a go on an alto.'[67] His earliest outings with the guitar were as a busker. Simon Crocker joined him on harmonica a few times on the streets of Aix and even, on a couple of occasions, near the chic harbour area of fashionable St Tropez. 'We just used to laugh because the whole thing was so funny,' says Simon. 'Nick sat on an upturned milk crate, some folk used to toss money but we didn't care.' Their repertoire was 'the stuff on the Tanworth tapes', covers of songs by Bert Jansch, Bob Dylan, Jackson C Frank, Dave Van Ronk, some blues standards, Michael Row The Boat Ashore, Dino Valenti's Get Together, a real mixed bag.

Nick had also begun to sing a song he'd learned from a fellow French language student in Aix. Guitarist and singer Robin Frederick was a 19-year-old from Miami Florida via Southern California, who performed a mixture of folk standards and some original compositions in the cabaret club where foreign students gathered. Writing in *Mojo* magazine nearly a quarter of a century later, she recalled how Nick had introduced himself one evening after a gig and asked if she would care to get together to play some songs. From then on Nick would appear regularly at Robin's flat and the two would while away the night playing guitar. Robin Frederick doesn't remember Nick playing any of his own songs either, just covers. She does recall him enjoying Changes by Phil Ochs and detects traces of it in Nick's own compositions, which she didn't hear until many years after his death. Another song she taught him was her own, somewhat prescient, Been Smokin' Too Long, which was thought to be a Nick Drake original until a home recording of it appeared on the *Time Of No Reply* album in 1986 and Robin Frederick stood up to claim it. Since then she has written extensively about Nick in magazines and on her website,[68] and has become the inevitable centre of speculation that she and Nick had an affair in Aix, an accusation she has always denied.

'We knew each other for only a short time,' she wrote in *Mojo*. 'I'm still not sure who I met; but then, that's what everyone says about him. Yet, for someone who was so elusive, he had an unmistakable presence that drew people to him. To put it bluntly, falling in love with Nick was a no-brainer and I promptly did; not that I ever let on, mind you. He was extraordinarily attractive and that, plus his natural quietness, made it easy to weave a web of fantasies around him.' For a clue about Robin Frederick's feelings for Nick listen to her composition Sandy Grey on John Martyn's first album *London*

Conversation or her own version on her website: 'Oh Sandy Grey, I thought I heard you say, You ain't heard one word that I've been speaking.' According to Robin, Sandy Grey is 'an indefinable, shifting shade – that was Nick to a T'.

So what about other girls in Aix? 'No, he didn't have a specific girlfriend,' says Simon Crocker, 'but there were girls. There was one I remember I was very keen on. And there was shagging!' 'Oh there were definitely girls,' recalls Jeremy Mason. 'I was madly keen on girls but part of my problem was that they found Nick a better bet!' However, both Simon and Jeremy paint a picture of Nick seeming to float above the carnal world of student sex, perhaps seeking more cerebral satisfaction, perhaps too shy to join in with his peers, or perhaps struggling to come to terms with the trauma of a childhood sexual experience. There was one incident when a female student from a well-to-do family got involved in group sex with a number of boys and took pleasure in recounting the story. His friends noticed that Nick was perturbed. He was clearly uncomfortable with this kind of behaviour and – in an echo of the story from Eagle House – he appeared to look down his nose at the participants.

This stand-offishness is what has given rise to the speculation that Nick was gay. Not so, say his friends from Marlborough and Aix. 'He was very shy and women came on to him though he was never the predator,' says Jeremy Mason. 'We were young, we were looking for a shag, but Nick wasn't like that – that doesn't make him gay, but it does make him that kind of person. We knew what gay boys were – there were "queers" at school – but it never occurred to me that Nick was that way inclined.'

Less ambiguous was Nick's growing appetite for drugs. 'He went from schoolboy to drug-taking musician' in a few months, says Jeremy Mason. 'He must have been taking more than I thought.' Nick probably took his first LSD trip in Aix. Certainly the lyrics of Clothes Of Sand, which dates from this period – 'to see the earth through painted eyes' – are suggestive of an interest in hallucinogenics: 'I remember vividly going back to the flat once and finding it barricaded,' recalls Jeremy Mason. 'He wouldn't have done that if he was just smoking pot. I don't know where he got it from but there was stuff going on. He had discussed taking drugs with my mother the summer before, along with a guy I knew who ended up in a Thai jail. It's an irony that people say drugs don't do any harm, but the two people I knew who took them are both dead!'

Nick was beginning to grow away from his old school friends. He was increasingly attracted to another group of English students who would have a big influence on his later life. Among the other upper-class refugees in the south of France was Roddy Llewellyn, who later had a much-publicised relationship with Princess Margaret. He recalls that Nick often had a big smile on his face but 'was very intense, a tortured soul'. Nick enjoyed the attention of well-connected socialites and Old Etonians like Julian Lloyd and Derek Fitzgerald, and the willowy debutantes who hovered round them. Ben Laycock and Nick Lewin were also part of a group that took Nick under its collective wing. Often crouched over his acoustic guitar, usually sipping red wine and always smoking, Nick became a kind of mascot for these super-rich English glitterati. And they acted as a conduit for him into a darker, more serious world of drug use.

This was the era when drugs meant experimentation, literally a 'trip' into a new world and new experiences. Normally that meant a cerebral or spiritual journey but for Nick Drake the spring of 1967 opened up the opportunity of a real journey to the modern mecca of hippy drug culture, Morocco. One day a souped-up Ford Cortina GT roared into Aix carrying Richard (Rick) Charkin, a former pupil of Haileybury School near Hertford, and a fellow student from Paris. Their plan was to drive south through General Franco's Spain and across the Mediterranean to Tangier. 'That was where you got the best pot,' says Richard Charkin. Jeremy Mason didn't join the expedition because he had a girlfriend visiting. But he helped persuade Nick to 'free up the bedroom'. There's a sense in both Jeremy Mason and Simon Crocker's reports of this period that Nick was beginning to drift away, both from them as close friends and from conventional student hedonism into a deeper quest. 'He went off with a different set,' says Jeremy Mason wistfully.

The trip – and that's what it was – sounds like a cross between *Three Men In A Boat* and *On The Road*: four young and impressionable English chaps on the hippy trail. With Rick's friend and Nick sharing the driving, and Rick Charkin and another now-forgotten student friend in the back, the four set off over the Pyrenees and into Andorra where the highly tuned Cortina struggled with the thin atmosphere. They drove across Spain day and night, rolling joints as they went and stopping only for a quick 'wow' at the Alhambra in Granada. In next to no time they were scoring some cheap Moroccan hashish on the quayside in Tangier. 'Actually it was probably weaker stuff than we could get back in England. I think they saw us coming,' says Richard Charkin. 'But we were too out of it to care!' A day or two later they were in Marrakech sipping coffee on the Djema El Fnaa as the muezzins called the faithful to prayer.

Marrakech is a city of powerful experiences, where the sounds, sights and smells of North Africa assault every sense. But what happened next must have been, in the jargon of the day, truly mind-blowing. Nick and his friends went for a meal in the smart French quarter of Marrakech. As they sat down they noticed the trademark floppy hat of celebrity photographer Cecil Beaton. With him were Mick Jagger, Keith Richards, Keith's girlfriend Anita Pallenberg and 'several other assorted Stones and hangers-on'. It's likely that Marianne Faithfull was also in the party because this was only weeks before the infamous Redlands drug bust that led to Keith and Mick's imprisonment for narcotics offences. Richard Charkin says that Nick and his friends were astonished. They'd come over 1,000 miles from home to immerse themselves in Moroccan culture, only to find themselves in a restaurant with the apostles of the counter-culture.

Despite the fact that Richard Charkin remembers his friend Nick Drake as 'shy', he tried to persuade him to play a song for The Stones on the acoustic guitar he had brought out with him because he didn't want to leave it behind in the cheap hotel. Fuelled by some cheap local wine, they told the rock-star party that they should hear their friend. 'We had to kick him quite hard – it wasn't him saying, "Oh, I'd like to go and impress that lot",' says Rick. 'We thought he could play but we didn't think he was that good – it was just a way of us getting to see the girls and say we'd met The Stones.' And so it was that The Rolling Stones sat and listened as 18-year-old Nick Drake serenaded them with a selection of Dylan and Donovan covers. With typical sangfroid Nick described the episode to his parents in a letter: 'We saw the Stones eating in a small restaurant and Bob, displaying once more his nerve, marched in and told them I wanted to play guitar for them … surprisingly enough they accepted this time so I went in and did them a few numbers. We in fact got quite chatty with them and it was quite interesting learning all the inside stories.' *Quite* interesting?

'Then someone suggested we drive to Chad,' recalls Richard Charkin. A glance at the atlas would have confirmed that the idea was foolish to the point of suicidal so, perhaps fortunately, they didn't make it very far. Long before they reached the Sahara Desert the Ford Cortina came off the road in the Atlas Mountains and rolled on to its side. Fortunately, all the passengers were safe, if a little shocked, and only too glad when a breakdown truck arrived to take them and the battered Cortina to Meknès. The problem now was that they had nowhere near enough money to repair the car. They were saved when it emerged that the garage mechanic thought these four upper-class Englishmen were actually The Rolling Stones, who had been featured in Moroccan newspapers. A deal was done whereby they would pose for before-and-after pictures of the car, which could be used by the garage as publicity shots. A week later, they were on their way home. After a lengthy and heart-stopping search at Moroccan customs, they limped back to Aix where Nick returned to the Residence Sextius, while Richard Charkin and his friend headed back to Paris to teach English. 'He was a good-looking sort of bloke, definitely shy, absolutely, but a nice guy, we liked him,' recalls Richard Charkin. 'We swapped addresses, but I didn't expect to see him again.'

In a sense none of his old friends saw Nick again after Aix. Whether it was the liberation of escape from Tanworth and the suffocation of family life, or the experimentation with and increasing reliance on drugs, or his growing confidence in his ability as a musician, the Nick Drake who travelled back to England in the summer of 1967 was a profoundly different character to the one who had left six months earlier.

A remarkable insight into his state of mind at this time comes from one of the few extant recordings of Nick's speaking voice. While he was back in Tanworth during the break between Aix and Cambridge, he went out to a society party and returned home in the small hours. He was drunk and probably stoned. As the sun came up over the Warwickshire countryside he switched on his tape recorder in the music room at Far Leys and began to mumble in an accent which to modern ears sounds uncannily like that of his soon-to-be Cambridge contemporary Prince Charles.[69]

He reports that he has 'enjoyed oneself' at the Maynard Mitchells although he has to 'make reservations because the people weren't particularly interesting.' He describes driving home drunk after his 'merry abandon' and finding himself on the wrong side of the road after a 'mental brainstorm' which made him imagine he was still in France. Then suddenly his language changes. 'In moments of stress' he whispers, 'one forgets so easily the lies, the truth and the pain.'

Acknowledging that he is wavering at this point, Nick goes on to describe how he's been playing the piano and hopes he hasn't woken anyone upstairs, and then embarks on a rambling discourse about the pleasures of watching the sun come up. A tree in Far Leys garden is green whereas it should be black 'before one goes to bed.' Seeing in the new day is both 'an achievement' and 'an experience'.

Whether he was dictating a message to a friend or simply talking to himself, the key passage is the one that starts with the light-hearted story about drunk-driving and suddenly spins into a vortex of depression. There is something at work here that goes deeper than the traditional ramblings of the adolescent drunk. The lies, the truth and the pain? Is Nick's subconscious starting to tell us something about his mental state in that crucial summer? This was the period of his life that gave birth to some of his most telling lyrics – 'a troubled cure for a troubled mind', 'this is the time of no reply', 'life is but a memory happened long ago'. These are the words of a wounded and grieving mind, not yet ready or perhaps able to cry out in the direct language of his later songs, but nursing something more corrosive than temporary teen angst.

3. Poor Boy, So Sorry for Himself

8. *Bryter Later*

FROM THE outset the marketing of Nick Drake's first album, *Five Leaves Left*, was a shambles. There was soon tension between Joe Boyd's Witchseason and Island Records, both feeling that the other was disorganised and uncommitted to this difficult new artist. An advertisement for Fairport Convention's *Unhalfbricking* LP appeared in the *Melody Maker* on July 5, 1969, which included a brief, slightly apologetic, mention of a forthcoming release by Nick Drake: 'Listen to the record for the great playing by Danny Thompson, Paul Harris and Richard Thompson and the amazing string arrangements – then you'll find out about the singer and his songs.' Review copies were sent to music journalists the same month and on July 26th, *Melody Maker* carried a paragraph that pointed out the Rizla reference in the title of the album and then damned Nick with the remarkable sentence, 'His debut album for Island is interesting.'

The album's release was delayed several times because of production and printing difficulties, and when it finally arrived in the shops in September there was no advertising campaign whatsoever. Just at the point where Nick needed maximum media profile, he was conspicuous in the pages of the music papers only by his absence. He was told that the plan was to let his music creep up on an audience, to let people discover him in their own time and avoid hype. But he must have guessed that this was also a self-serving strategy for Witchseason and Island, neither of whom had major-label publicity budgets. To make things worse, the gatefold sleeve of *Five Leaves Left*, though impressive, contained no explanatory notes or biographical material. It also transposed two songs in the running order,[70] mistakenly called Three Hours 'Sundown', and included an unrecorded verse in the lyrics of River Man. Gabrielle Drake has told the story many times of how her brother came into her bedroom in her Battersea flat and tossed a copy of his debut album on her bed without comment. She sees his actions as signs of modesty and diffidence, but with hindsight it's likely that he wasn't completely satisfied with the record or its careless packaging.

Things might have been manageable if Nick had developed a fan base through live appearances. It was always possible for acoustic guitar troubadours like Bert Jansch, John Martyn and Ralph McTell to sell a few albums because their supporters in the folk clubs were waiting for a new release by artists they already knew on stage. But no one had ever heard of Nick Drake. Reports of his live performances in Cambridge suggest that, while he was no showman, he did enjoy playing live. But by the summer of 1969, something had changed. He may have started to suffer from self-doubt after the Caius May Ball in June where his gentle, introspective chamber music had failed to quieten a boisterous student crowd. He may have felt that the songs on his debut album should only be performed with strings and that he could no longer do them justice as a soloist. Either way, friends and colleagues began to notice a reluctance to play live, which had the makings of a phobia.

Nick did agree to record a solo session for BBC Radio 1. On August 5th Joe Boyd's assistant Anthea Joseph collected him and his trusty Guild M20 guitar from his temporary digs at 3 Aldridge Road Villas in Notting Hill where he was sharing with a hippy girl and her pet monkey, which one witness says, 'shat everywhere'. They travelled a mile or so to the BBC's live music studios in a former ice rink on Delaware Road, Maida Vale, where, according to the curious administrative practice of the day Nick recorded a 'trial broadcast' that would be 'put before the Popular Music (Sound) Production Panel and so assessed for future broadcast'. The session form, which still exists in the BBC archives, doesn't record what the panel made of this 'vocal/guitarist', but Nick must have passed the test because the three songs he recorded in Studio 5 – Cello Song, River Man and Time Of No Reply – were broadcast the following night, Wednesday, August 6th, in John Peel's short-lived Wednesday-evening 'rock and progressive music' show between 8:15 and 9:15. The producer, Pete Ritzema, who also recorded Jimi Hendrix's first radio session, was disappointed: 'he left gaps for the string arrangements while he'd just strum away. I thought he would be a folkie and improvise but he wasn't up for that'.[71] Most of the subtleties of the performance would have been lost anyway on the listeners to Radio 1, which was broadcast only on AM[72] in those days. Reception across most of the UK was impossible after dark.

Pete Ritzema noted that Nick Drake was 'a gloomy fellow, very, very quiet'. In an interview between the session tracks John Peel asked Nick what he'd been up to recently. 'Wasting my time in Cambridge' was the answer. Something was happening in London to that shy but affable member of the Loungers. Island's A&R manager at the time, Muff Winwood, has no doubt what was going on: 'I remember waking Nick up at his grotty flat in Notting Hill. I had to make friends with the bloke downstairs to let me in. Nick used to stay up 'til six smoking dope and then my job was to get him out of his stinky bed.' A former member of the successful Spencer Davis Group and brother of Steve, Muff Winwood was experienced in the ways of the music business. He was used to musicians who were 'out of it' on drugs, booze or just plain laziness. But Nick made him angry. 'I lost count of the number of TV sessions and radio sessions we missed because he was so untogether. It was totally frustrating. He was a complete pain in the arse, drove me up the wall.'

In the circumstances, Joe Boyd's big idea to promote Nick was quite extraordinary. Question: how do you draw attention to a quiet and introverted musician with a profound and growing reluctance to play live? Answer: put him on stage in one of the biggest and most prestigious venues in the country in front of two and a half thousand expectant folk-rock fans. On September 24th, Joe's biggest act was headlining London's cavernous Royal Festival Hall. Ticket prices for 'Fairport Convention ... and Friends' ranged from 25 shillings to 8 shillings[73] to see their classic line-up with Sandy Denny, Richard Thompson and Ashley Hutchings, augmented by the exhilarating fiddler Dave Swarbrick. Nick Drake was given the daunting task of opening for the Fairports, but it turned into more of a warm-down than a warm-up.

It's perhaps no surprise that Joe Boyd has described the audience as 'mesmerised' and Nick's performance as 'brilliant'. But other witnesses saw it differently. Nick simply didn't have the stagecraft to command the attention of such a big auditorium. With only one guitar[74] he needed lengthy breaks for re-tuning between songs. He didn't have the confidence to fill the gaps with stories or even the most basic introductions. And the PA was so quiet that people at the back of the hall couldn't hear him at all. Even his parents, who had turned up without telling him – 'because we were afraid it would absolutely throw Nick' – were aware that his performance was lacking. Molly told the BBC's David Barber that 'Nick just came in, played, got up, went out, you know, there was no showmanship of any sort.'[75]

A few days later, on October 4th, the influential *New Musical Express* finally published its review of *Five Leaves Left*. A writer identified only as GC wasn't impressed. 'I'm sorry I can't be more enthusiastic because he obviously has a not inconsiderable amount of talent, but there is not nearly enough variety on this debut LP to make it entertaining.' Comparing Nick's vocal style to that of Peter Sarstedt, the generously moustachioed one-hit wonder, whose Where Do You Go To My Lovely had been a number one hit earlier in the year, he wrote that Nick's songs 'lack Sarstedt's penetration and arresting quality'. Criticism doesn't come much harsher than that. The influential *Oz* magazine didn't review the album at all, although it did find room for an article on Island's next release, *Kip Of The Serenes* by the equally unknown Dr Strangely Strange.

With press coverage limited and radio play non-existent,[76] Nick was finally packed off on a series of folk club gigs. On the very same day that the *NME* review appeared, the *Melody Maker* small ads contained notice that Nick Drake, supported by The Folkomnibus, would be appearing that night at the Upper Room Folk Club in the Goodwill To All on Headstone Lane in Harrow, north London. Just weeks after the release of his remarkable debut album, Nick was playing to 30 folk fans in the upstairs room of a suburban pub. Bruce Fursman, then aged 16, played mandolin with the support band. He remembers Nick arriving on his own, probably by cab, while The Folkomnibus were on stage. As they finished, Nick applauded, joked that 'you've played my set guys', which suggests that he was still including some covers in his own show, and then asked to have a pick on Bruce's mandolin. After a break for drinks from the downstairs bar, Nick 'sat hunched-up on a chair, in a jacket, white shirt, very humble, no mic, very grown up,' says Bruce Fursman. 'The atmosphere was reverential.' His colleague in The

Folkomnibus, Andy Whetstone, recalls Nick's playing as 'very accurate' and Bruce Fursman thought his material was 'remarkable'. Like many people since, he was 'slightly miffed when Nick became famous – I thought this is *my* music!'

But other gigs were less successful. Nick played The Haworth pub in Hull supporting Michael Chapman,[77] who remembers that the hard-core northern folk audience were unappreciative of Nick's gentle, hypnotic songs. 'He didn't introduce any of them; he didn't say a word the entire evening. It was actually quite painful to watch,' he told *Pynk Moon* magazine. Worse was to follow at Guest, Keen & Nettlefold's social club in Smethwick, Birmingham, where Nick was booked to play to rowdy steel workers who just wanted to party. Joe Boyd (his agent as well as his manager and record producer) may have hoped that booking Nick into such unsuitable venues would build his confidence, but it was a disaster. 'The more he didn't say anything, the louder people talked and then he would whisper his vocals and eventually he just got up and walked off stage.' At least Joe Boyd does now admit that mistakes were made. 'I don't think I did a very good job', he told Belgian radio, 'I was faced with a problem and I didn't come up with a solution.' What had started as stage fright was rapidly turning into deep-seated paranoia.

It didn't help that Nick was now smoking industrial quantities of cannabis, a drug notorious for inducing lethargy, apathy and paranoia. It was also during his first few months in London that he met Dave,[78] an East End villain and well-known drug dealer on the underground scene who lived with his wife and baby in Holland Park. Dave could supply mandrax, nembutal, LSD, hash oil, in fact any uppers or downers, barbiturates or hallucinogens his musician friends requested. Linda Thompson remembers that Nick would attend Dave's Friday-night poker sessions and he became such a good customer, and friend, that Dave bought him a car, telling the other members of the circle that 'he's gotta 'av' wheels'. It was also around this time that Nick first experimented with heroin. On one occasion his Cambridge friend Brian Wells was taken to meet some of the ex-debs and socialites of Nick's Chelsea set. 'He introduced me to Alice Ormsby-Gore, who was living with Eric Clapton at the time, in some Chelsea flat full of super-intelligent articulate people of a kind I'd never met before. Alice was smoking dope and said, "Sooooooo lovely to see you Nick", and he was clearly very much in with them and there was a sense of them being slightly in awe of him.' Alice Ormsby-Gore, who died in 1995, was notorious within London's demi-monde, as a heroin user, and it seems likely that Nick tried smack for the first time with her, snorting it like Clapton rather than injecting it. Today, an artist exhibiting Nick's problem might be dispatched to The Priory, but this was the late 1960s and early 1970s, an era when any amount of drug abuse was tolerated, even encouraged, by people who should have known better.

Some friends, like Brian Wells, argue that Nick's drug use must have been minimal because he didn't have enough money to sustain a habit. But what money he did have was being spent on something, certainly neither clothes nor rent. Everyone who knew him in 1969 and 1970 recalls that he never had any money and wore the same jacket, jeans and zip boots all the time.[79] And he was living a nomadic life at this time, crashing with friends and sleeping on floors. He had a room whenever he wanted it in Alex Henderson's flat on Edith Terrace in Chelsea. Occasionally he stayed with his sister, who had moved into a smart house in Campden Hill Gardens in Kensington with her South African boyfriend Louis de Wet, but Brian Wells recalls that the irascible de Wet wasn't too enamoured of his girlfriend's hippy brother. 'Nick and I went round and Louis opened the door and yelled, "Gabrielle, friends of yours are here." He was clearly not pleased that we'd come and Gabrielle came to the door and said, "Are you all right?", but we decided not to go in because de Wet was clearly not in the mood for us visiting.'

Eventually Joe Boyd decided to bring some stability into Nick's life and paid for him to take a flat with a telephone. He moved his few possessions into the ground floor of 112 Haverstock Hill on the corner of Parkhill Road in London's Belsize Park. Drake fans who make the pilgrimage today are disappointed to see that the grand semi-detached Victorian house where Nick lived has been demolished and replaced with a functional 1980s apartment block, but you can get an idea of the building Nick inhabited by looking at 114 and 116 next door. After spells in Battersea and then Kensington with Gabrielle, in Notting Hill, in Chelsea and in Earl's Court, Belsize Park was to become the nearest thing Nick would ever have to a home in London. Photographs taken by Keith Morris show that it was poorly decorated and very sparsely furnished, but he denies that it was squalid. 'It was spartan, quite minimalist, but it wasn't a squat. It was clean,' he laughs, 'sort of feng shui before its time!'

Haverstock Hill, a short walk from the Chalk Farm underground station, where one imagines Nick 'sailing downstairs to the Northern Line, watching the shine of the shoes',[80] would become the inspiration for his second album. Although *Five Leaves Left* had sold poorly – probably no more than 3,000 copies – Joe Boyd, who had produced and released no less than three Fairport Convention albums during 1969, was keen to get something else into the shops as soon as possible to build on what momentum there was. And Nick was anxious to move on from the pastoral sound of his first record and reflect the new urban landscapes and lifestyle that he was fitting into. 'The plan was to make an up, good, happy album,' says Robert Kirby, who was engaged to write not just string but also brass arrangements for some of the new songs. 'It was more of a pop sound, I suppose,' admits Joe Boyd. 'I imagined it as more commercial.'

Once again the sessions took place in Sound Techniques studio with John Wood engineering and Joe Boyd 'sitting upstairs reading the baseball results'.[81] Nick had agreed with Joe that the new album needed to have a fuller 'rock band' sound so, for the first time since he left Marlborough, he started rehearsals with bass and drums. The members of Fairport Convention and their families were living in an old pub called The Angel in Little Hadham near Bishop's Stortford in Essex and Nick was sent up there for a few days to routine some of his new songs with bass player Dave Pegg and drummer Dave Mattacks. 'Nick was never happy when we were doing it,' recalls Dave Pegg, 'he never expressed any opinion, there was no eye contact, he never said "You played great, thanks."'

Joe Boyd has admitted that Nick wasn't entirely happy with the sessions. In a telling interview in 2004 he said, 'I think that once he began to hear the record coming together, Robert writing for horns in a much more aggressive texture, I think – well, I don't know, we never really talked about it. But ... he felt that it was too arranged, too produced, too many other personalities, I guess.'[82] It's surely significant that Joe and Nick 'never really talked about it'. The song Poor Boy was a case in point. Early unaccompanied recordings of it reveal Nick's aching insecurity and his deep disillusionment with everything going on around him. It's a haunting and fragile song, but on the record, it's swamped by a Delaney & Bonnie or Leon Russell-style arrangement featuring Chris McGregor from The Brotherhood Of Breath on piano and session singers Pat (PP) Arnold and Doris Troy. McGregor was involved because Joe Boyd was producing the first BOB album at Sound Techniques and the South African simply turned up for his own session on the wrong day.

Also working with Joe Boyd at the time was John Cale, recently departed from the legendary Velvet Underground. The two of them were co-producing Nico's classic *Desertshore* album and Dave Pegg would see them 'hanging out in the control room' at Sound Techniques. 'We weren't really hippies,' he says, 'so we thought all these druggy, freaky people were a bit strange.' When John Cale heard Nick Drake's music he was enchanted. 'He was a very quiet guy. It was very difficult to figure out what was going on in his mind. He made music with a real sensuality – very different from English folk music.'[83] So he persuaded Joe Boyd to let him play on the album. For a couple of days in the spring of 1970, Cale moved into Nick's Belsize Park flat and worked on two of his best songs, Fly and Northern Sky. Joe Boyd remembers Nick being overawed by John Cale's fame and phenomenal musicality: 'he was kinda trailing in his wake. I said, "Are you happy with this, Nick", "Yeh, yeh, I guess so yeh, yeh."' For Fly, Cale invented beautiful understated viola and harpsichord parts, which perfectly complemented the mood of the song. He gave Northern Sky a dramatic new middle section and added celeste, piano and Hammond organ, giving the recording a subtlety that Robert Kirby's full-blown arrangements didn't quite match on some of the other songs.

Those few days with John Cale may also have had another impact on Nick. Cale has admitted in his biography that he was using heroin at this time and Nick's friend Brian Wells confirms that Nick was showing an interest in the drug, so it seems likely that smack played a part in the brief but highly productive Cale/Drake relationship. Older friends had certainly begun to notice a big change in Nick's personality. Jeremy Mason, his close friend from Marlborough College and Aix-en-Provence, had started work at the auctioneers Christie's. He met Nick for drinks one evening in the Princess Of Wales pub, now a smart French restaurant called Le Colombier at 145 Dovehouse St in Chelsea, and became convinced that Nick was 'using drugs to enhance the creative process'. He found their old friendship difficult to re-ignite. 'He disapproved of me by then. My path was no less honourable than his, but it didn't involve smoking dope and falling over. He was aloof and on a couple of occasions he did make me feel uncool.' Jeremy left some keys at Nick's flat but when Nick returned them to Christie's the following day 'he just dropped them at reception, he didn't call to say hello'. Rick Charkin, a veteran of the 1967 Morocco trip, went round to Belsize Park one afternoon and saw Nick through the window sitting and staring at the wall, quite motionless. 'I couldn't raise him,' he says, 'I think it was a little bit of the drug thing and a little bit of him – he was always a bit like that.'

Nick decided that his second album would be called *Bryter Layter*. Echoing a familiar phrase from TV and radio weather forecasts, he gave it an olde worlde spelling, according to Robert Kirby, 'as a bit of a joke', perhaps remembering the membership card of the Cambridge Loungers. But it was also an ironic title. The lyrics could have left no one in any doubt that their author was going downhill fast. He hated London where, in the words of his songs, he 'talked with neighbours only' and people thought him 'either weird or lonely'. Things were moving too fast. He cursed where he came from. He'd fallen down and was now sitting 'on the ground in your way'. He was a 'poor boy, so sorry for himself'. Anguished words of self-pity and isolation were pouring out of him. But was anyone listening? The only interpretation can be that Nick's defensiveness erected a wall that even his friends couldn't penetrate. His sister has said that Nick had a skin too few. Perhaps he had a skin too many.

* * *

ONE CHINK of light amid Nick's increasing separation and desolation was Joe Boyd's decision to record a sampler album to promote the work of the songwriters he had signed to Warlock Publishing. He hoped that by setting the songs of John Martyn, Beverley Martyn, Mike Heron of The Incredible String Band, Ed Carter from the Beach Boys band, and Nick Drake, in a pop context, he could persuade some famous artists to cover their songs on big-selling albums. Perhaps Nick might be able to make real money. The session for the Warlock sampler, at DJM Studios on New Oxford Street in London, featured Traffic's Jim Capaldi on drums, Fotheringay's Pat Donaldson[84] on bass, Fairport Convention's Simon Nicol on guitar, Linda Peters (soon to marry Richard Thompson) and a young pianist from Pinner called Reg Dwight who, like Nick, had recently made his first solo album, under the name Elton John. The arrangements were by Del Newman, who went on to define the hugely popular Cat Stevens sound on albums like *Tea For The Tillerman*.[85]

Elton's versions of Way To Blue, Day Is Done, Time Has Told Me and Saturday Sun sound like they've come straight off the *Elton John* album or *Tumbleweed Connection*. In fact when he heard them for the first time in 35 years, he told me, 'I just played them to Davey, my guitarist, and he said, "I can't remember you writing these!" They really do sound like I might have written them.' Before the session Elton was already familiar with *Five Leaves Left* through his friend Muff Winwood. 'I loved that album so much,' he says, 'the melodies, the non-conformity of the songs (they're not just verse/chorus/verse), their bleakness, their beauty, very personal, very moving … I found solace in them. There was no one like that in the UK. He was just as good as Jeff Buckley and Rufus Wainwright.' Elton made the songs his own but, as guitar-based compositions, were they difficult to play on the piano? 'No, they suited me; they sound like they were written on the piano.'

Legend has it that when Elton sold his vinyl collection to raise money for his AIDS Foundation he kept a copy of the Warlock sampler. 'Sadly not true,' he says, 'I really regret it now. It's been great to hear them again; it wasn't a job, it was a labour of love.' There are reputed to be just seven vinyl white labels in existence, although there are many bootlegs in circulation. The last genuine copy sold for $3,000 on eBay in 2004.

* * *

AT THE beginning of 1970, Nick was pushed into another round of punishing live appearances. On January 24th he played to an unreceptive crowd at Ewell Technical College, supporting Atomic Rooster and fellow public schoolboys Genesis. Then on February 21st, he was back on London's South Bank opening what was billed as 'A Concert of Contemporary Music' with his friends and Island labelmates John and Beverley Martyn at the Queen Elizabeth Hall. His set included two then unreleased songs, Hazey Jane I and Things Behind The Sun, and at least one member of the audience was impressed. Herman Gilligan, a young folk fan from west London recalls that Nick 'shambled on and said, "This is a song about Mayfair"; he was great, lovely songs, John Martyn was disappointing by comparison.' But most of the audience of 1,500 was unmoved. Later, John Martyn told the BBC that Nick 'was cripplingly nervous. I mean, he was distraught before the gig. It was rather embarrassing in fact to see him. He was distinctly uncomfortable on stage. I mean, the music was fine, but he just didn't like being there at all.' Island's press officer, David Sandison, was less forgiving. 'He was embarrassing because he was very gauche, and there were long pauses between the numbers because he was either re-tuning or thinking about it.'

The following month, Nick's friend from Cambridge Iain Cameron, who had played flute for him at the Caius May Ball, called him with an idea. One of Iain's mates, Alec Reid, was now a producer at BBC Radio 2 and Iain had asked him if he would book Nick for a session on the 'Night Ride' programme, which went out between midnight and 2am. Reid knew *Five Leaves Left* and readily agreed, so Nick and Iain turned up at Studio S2 in the sub-basement of Broadcasting

House for what turned out to be his second and last radio session. It was broadcast during the 'Night Ride' programme in the early hours of April 13, 1970. 'His diffidence was now evident personally but not yet professionally or musically,' says Iain Cameron. 'Talking to him was strange, you could feel the distance and lack of confidence, but at one point he saw a celeste in the studio and just sat down and played it on Saturday Sun.' Iain didn't see much of his old friend after that. 'I did go round to Belsize Park once and he offered me a cup of tea, but he couldn't get it together to make it.'

Also in March 1970 Nick embarked on another tour, this time supporting Sandy Denny's new band Fotheringay. He was due to play five more gigs: Birmingham Town Hall (March 16th), Leicester De Montfort Hall (March 18th), Manchester Free Trade Hall (March 20th), Bristol Colston Hall (March 22nd) and London Royal Festival Hall (March 30th). To make his humiliation complete, Nick was followed on stage every night by a second support act that exuded all the stagecraft and humour he so obviously lacked: The Humblebums, featuring Gerry Rafferty and the famous raconteur Billy Connolly. 'After three concerts,' says Joe Boyd, 'he called me and he said, "I can't do this any more".'

There were a few other attempts. On May 8th he was coaxed on to the bill at an all-nighter at Bedford College, possibly because his friend John Martyn was there and also because his old favourite from schooldays, Graham Bond, was playing. A few days later he played an open-air concert in Yorkshire, headlined by fellow Island artists Free, and on

June 25th the audience at Ewell Technical College witnessed Nick Drake's last ever concert performance. Ralph McTell was headlining: 'Nick was monosyllabic. At that particular gig he was very shy. He did the first set and something awful must have happened. He was doing his song, Fruit Tree, and walked off halfway through it. Just left the stage.'

During late 1969 and early 1970 Nick could be seen on the more intimate folk circuit in London, at Bunjie's on Litchfield Street, the Troubadour in Earl's Court and notably at the famous Les Cousins club opposite the Pillars of Hercules pub at 49 Greek Street in Soho. Patrons went downstairs off the street into one of two smoky rooms at Cousins. On the left was a coffee bar with a small wooden stage about two feet high and measuring six foot square. There was only one electrical socket, one microphone and no air conditioning. The audience sat on the floor, and when the room was crowded perched on the stage with their backs to the act.

Herman Gilligan saw Nick at the bar one night and introduced himself. 'Excuse me are you Nick Drake? You're brilliant.' Nick was uncommunicative even with a fervent fan. 'He didn't know what to say. He had no small talk,' recalls Gilligan, 'so I asked him if he knew who was on the record player and he just said "The Band" and walked off.' Another night, John Martyn rushed into Cousins and pushed his way on stage so he could introduce his friend. 'Nick lumbered on,' according to Gilligan, 'head down, sang each song, there was a polite "thank you", but he didn't introduce the songs, there was no eye contact. People like Al Stewart,

John Martyn, Roy Harper, contextualised their music – Nick didn't bother.' However this clearly suited the confined and reverential space of Cousins better than the theatres and sports halls he'd been playing to promote his record. Gilligan describes the gigs as 'ethereal and soothing. His guitar technique was extraordinary, I just couldn't understand how he did it. My mate and I were quite stunned afterwards riding home to Hayes on my Honda 50.'

In an evocative memoir for *Pynk Moon* magazine, Brian Cullman, who played at a Cousins all-nighter with Nick, recalled the impact that this introverted, stooping guitarist had on him. 'His shyness and awkwardness were almost transcendent. A tall man, his clothes – black corduroy jacket and pants, frayed white shirt – hung around him like bed clothes after a particularly bad night's sleep. He sat on a small stool, hunched tight over a tiny Guild guitar, beginning songs and, halfway through, forgetting where he was and stumbling back to the start of that song, or beginning an entirely different song, which he would then abandon mid-way through if he remembered the remainder of the first. He sang away from the microphone, mumbled and whispered, all with a sense of precariousness and doom. It was like being at the bedside of a dying man who wants to tell you a secret, but who keeps changing his mind at the last minute. There was a new song that he sang that night, that he kept starting and stopping, never completing; he finally just sang the opening lines over and over again: "Do you curse where you came from/Do you swear in the night?" [Hazey Jane I]. It was chilling and morbidly fascinating. No one took their eyes off him for a second – there was a real sense of keeping him there with our gaze and attention, that if we looked away, however briefly, he might disappear, or forget that we were there and go to sleep.'

Another folk guitarist who played many times with Nick in this era was the Australian Ross Grainger. His recollection is that Nick's set in 1969 contained most of the songs from his third album, which wouldn't appear until 1972. 'In fact, Nick played a number of songs he never recorded or the versions that were recorded were very different to the ones he played live. I Was Made To Love Magic, The Thoughts Of Mary Jane and Tow The Line were the songs he played the most. He would only play songs like River Man when he was sure he had the audience's attention.' He played a few covers too including Yonder Comes The Blues, popularised by Stefan Grossman, and John Lee Hooker's Rent House Boogie. Ross Grainger and Nick actually appeared as a duo one night at the Troubadour off Old Brompton Road. 'Four of the songs we played were Man Of Constant Sorrow, The Water Is Wide, All My Trials and The Gypsy Rover. We also did one of Nick's songs that he never got around to recording. It was called Go Your Way And I'll Just Follow.'

However, even a friend and fan like Ross Grainger concedes that Nick was rarely a successful performer. 'Audiences were divided over Nick,' he says, 'the majority were not into his introspective style of music. There were occasions when he thought he wasn't going down well and it seemed to put him off. When I saw he wasn't being well received I would spend some time later reassuring him. He was, I guess, just too sensitive for the rough and tumble of the music business.'

If live performances weren't the answer to Nick's lack of success, there was perhaps still a chance he could make a living as a songwriter. In his role as Nick's publisher, Joe Boyd was trying hard to get his songs covered by established artists. The Warlock sampler featuring Elton John had failed to excite any interest, but there was one piece of good news during 1970. The Jamaican ska and blue beat singer Millie, whose My Boy Lollipop had reached number one on both sides of the Atlantic in 1964, recorded Nick's Mayfair for her album *Time Will Tell*, and Trojan Records issued it as a single. The song dated back to 1968 and Robert Kirby, who arranged the strings for Millie's version, had made a recording of Nick singing it in his college room, which emerged on the 2004 compilation *Made To Love Magic*. Unfortunately Millie's single and album disappeared without troubling either the charts or Nick's bank account.

Undaunted, Joe Boyd had another idea. He came into Sound Techniques one day announcing that he'd just flown back from Paris, where the legendary chanteuse Françoise Hardy had told him she was interested in recording some of Nick's material. Within days, Joe was back in Paris with the young producer and arranger Tony Cox and a very taciturn Nick Drake. 'He was painfully shy, terribly reserved,' says Tony Cox. The three of them went to Mme Hardy's sumptuous apartment on the Ile St Louis and had what Cox describes as 'a very odd meeting. She spoke only faltering English, Nick didn't say a word and although there was a vague promise that Nick might write some songs for her in the future, nothing was resolved at all.' Cox went on to produce two Françoise Hardy albums, neither of which included any of Nick's songs.

* * *

ON NOVEMBER 1, 1970, just in time to get swallowed up in the pre-Christmas release schedule, 22-year-old Nick Drake's second album, *Bryter Layter*, was released by Island. Astonishingly, the marketing was as bad, if not worse than it had been for his first. Five months earlier Keith Morris had been commissioned to take some shots for the sleeve. He remembers that the sessions were less spontaneous than those for *Five Leaves Left* and that Nick was exhibiting signs of being under pressure to compromise. They went first to Regent's Canal near Keith Morris's home and shot a series of black-and-white portraits with a guitar and a big book, but Joe Boyd turned them down. They tried again on a site that has since been redeveloped in New Cross, south London, overlooking the derelict docklands on the River Thames. It was a sunny June day, but Keith spent hours in the darkroom exposing the background three or four times more than the figure of Nick to make it look, as he put it, 'gloomy'. Later Joe Boyd commissioned Keith Morris to take a picture for the rear sleeve so, after dark one evening, he took Nick up to the newly built A40 Westway in Paddington, near his home, and shot another delayed exposure, reminiscent of the running man on *Five Leaves Left*. This time Nick is looking away from the camera as an out-of-focus car speeds past him.

Joe Boyd liked these pictures more but, to Keith Morris's chagrin, decided to approach Nigel Waymouth to shoot a cover portrait. Waymouth, a good personal friend of Boyd's, was the founder of the famous 1960s boutique Granny Takes A Trip and, with Michael English, had been half of Hapshash & The Coloured Coat, the designers of those psychedelic posters for UFO and Middle Earth events that adorned students' walls everywhere. Nick probably felt at ease because he knew Waymouth's girlfriend Victoria Yorke[86] very well through his Chelsea connections. But the result was wretched. Waymouth posed Nick in a Georgian stick-back chair, reputed to have once belonged to Charles Dickens, with a Guild M20 guitar.[87] In front of Nick he put a pair of blue suede brothel creepers. 'It's awful,' says Keith Morris, 'the whole thing says "loser".' Nick's portrait is set in a deep pink oval and surrounded by the most lurid violet of the sort used by cheap compilation albums. It was quite out of character with the music contained and must rank as one of the least appropriate sleeve designs in rock and pop history. There was another typographical error too – Robert Kirby was credited with 'bass' arrangements instead of 'brass'. Nick Drake fans, myself among them, were shocked by the new image. It did nothing to broaden his appeal but must have cost him sales among what small market he did have. As 1970 drew to a close, Nick Drake's career was no further forward than it had been two years earlier when he left Cambridge.

9. Pink Moon

DISAPPOINTED, disillusioned and despondent, Nick spent the winter of 1970/71 in his cold ground-floor flat, venturing out only to play an occasional folk club gig to make some money to buy drugs. Having turned his back on his family and many of his friends, he turned in on himself, blaming his own lack of confidence for the parlous state of his career, but unable to do anything about it. His mother Molly told Swedish radio that 'he just had one pair of shoes, which was completely worn out. He wouldn't have anything different. He wanted to be totally without material possessions at all, I think. This was a very bad time. He once said to me that everything started to go wrong from the Hampstead time on, and I think that was when things started to go wrong.'[88]

Bryter Layter's initial release was barely noticed. There were no reviews in music papers and, in spite of the urgings of Island's record plugger Garrell Redfearn, Nick was adamant that he either wouldn't or couldn't promote the record with live gigs, radio sessions or even press interviews. Still smoking what his friend and collaborator Robert Kirby describes as 'unbelievable amounts of cannabis', he was beginning to exhibit the first signs of psychosis. In those innocent times, the heads and freaks of bohemian London may have had a vague inkling that smoking joints and getting high could lead to temporary apathy, but they weren't bothered about longer-term effects. Dope was cool – unlike drink, which made straight people violent. Smoking was creative. It was mind-expanding. It was harmless. Not until many years later did scientists begin to prove a link between cannabis and schizophrenia.

Schizophrenia doesn't only mean split personality. Among its other symptoms[89] are: lack of emotion (the inability to enjoy activities as much as before); low energy (sitting around and sleeping much more than normal); lack of interest in life, low motivation; affective flattening (a blank, blunted facial expression, or less lively facial or physical movements); alogia (difficulty in speaking or inability to speak); lack of interest or ability to socialise with other people; inability to make friends or keep friends, or not caring to have friends; and social isolation (spending most of the day alone or with close family only). From an early age Nick could be withdrawn and uncommunicative and by 1972 he was exhibiting all of the symptoms of schizophrenia. This is not to say that he became a recluse overnight, but the first signs of the illness that eventually overwhelmed him were already there.

Alongside the mental problems, Nick was also suffering from real physical discomfort. Sometime during 1970 he began to experience pains in his back and groin, which were eventually diagnosed as kidney stones, a complaint that can sometimes cause acute pain, particularly in someone who isn't eating or drinking properly. Nick's familiar stoop became more pronounced as a result of his suffering, which was only eased when he was prescribed drugs to lessen the pain. It's unlikely that his doctor had any idea about the cocktail of other pharmaceuticals his patient was ingesting at the time.

The singer Linda Thompson (then Linda Peters), who had first met Nick while she was Joe Boyd's girlfriend, enjoyed what she calls 'a short and sweet romance' with Nick during 1971. 'It was lovely to be with him,' she says. 'He played guitar and we listened to records. If he didn't like something, he'd just get up and take the needle off the record and I'd keep playing stuff until I found something he did like. Art Tatum, Miles Davis, The Incredible String Band, Dudu Pukwana – yes, he loved Dudu – Chris McGregor, and of course he was very keen on Françoise Hardy.' Linda never visited Nick's home in Belsize Park. She and Nick always met in the flat in Holland Park that she shared with a vegan yoga instructor who was also 'enchanted by Nick'. They were part of a very promiscuous scene where, as Linda says, 'if a guy gave you a light for your fag it seemed churlish not to sleep with him'.

But Nick couldn't throw himself wholeheartedly into the bed-hopping. Just as in Aix, where he had appeared scornful of sexual over-indulgence, he was always distant, never able to commit himself to a physical relationship. 'No, we never slept together,' says Linda, 'we were clinchy and he stayed over, but it was very odd that it wasn't a full sexual thing. He went out with my friend Susie Watson Taylor, but that was just movies and cuddles and playing music too; I think it was the same with all of us. Whatever he was, he wasn't what we'd call red-blooded, definitely not.'

One of the most attractive women on the London music scene, Linda had other fish to fry. 'On the romantic front I thought, "I've got Richard Thompson waiting in the wings so you can bugger off mate, you're not putting any effort into this at all." I was incredibly cavalier about it, you know, this guy's lovely and I'm mad about him but obviously nothing's going to happen and at that age you think, "Oh it must be me", but he was like that with men too. He wasn't overly friendly with anyone. He was still adorable, it wasn't apathy, he didn't mean to ignore you, it was the just the way he was.'

Nick had always been more comfortable with the elements than with flesh and blood humanity. From the beginning his songs dealt with the sun, the moon, the sea, the sky, the seasons, caves, sand and mountains. His friend and fellow guitarist Ross Grainger remembers standing in the corner of Les Cousins folk club discussing other performers. 'I would ask Nick what he thought of who was on. He wouldn't criticise them straight out, but would say "life isn't that easy" and "things are more complicated than that".' Grainger sensed the fatalism in Nick. 'His philosophy was not just pessimistic, it was deterministic. We are the unwitting victims of tide, tempest and situations, much like Shakespeare suggested. There's more than a bit of Shakespeare in Nick. "To be or not to be" was very much the question for Nick, but the answer lay with the fates, the "Ides of March", or in the stars and not as John Lennon and co suggested, with ourselves surrendering to peace, love and good vibes.'

James Lovelock's theory of Gaia – 'we now see that the air, the ocean and the soil are much more than a mere environment for life; they are a part of life itself'[90] – was a big influence on Nick's thinking. Ross Grainger recalls discussing Lovelock's ideas with Nick and describes him as 'a modern pagan. He once said to me that it is not just us that lives and breathes, so does the earth and everything else'. Grainger confirms that Nick was as fascinated by the supernatural as he was bored by conventional life. 'We often discussed spirits, Stonehenge, ley lines and the little people. We used to discuss these kinds of things for hours.' Grainger refutes the idea that Nick was difficult to talk to. 'He just didn't want to discuss musical power games, record contracts and politics, and neither did he want to hurt anyone's feelings.'

Suddenly, Nick was snapped out of his slough of despond by the news that Island and Witchseason had decided to have another go at marketing *Bryter Layter*. Joe Boyd was convinced that it could sell in America, but to persuade a record company to release it there, he had to demonstrate that Nick's music was popular in Britain. So in March 1971, the album was re-promoted. Copies were sent out to the music papers and the initial signs were good. *Record Mirror* reviewer 'LG' wrote, 'A beautiful guitarist – clean and with perfect timing – accompanied by soft, beautiful arrangements by Robert Kirby. Nick isn't the world's top singer, but he's written fantastic numbers that suit strings marvellously. Definitely one of the prettiest (and that counts!) and most impressive albums I've heard. Remember what Mason Williams did with Classical Gas? A similar concept here, but Nick does it better – it's refined. Happy, sad, very moving.'

In *Sounds* magazine the renowned music journalist Jerry Gilbert singled out Joe Boyd and Robert Kirby for special praise and called *Bryter Layter* 'a superb album. On their own merits, the songs of Nick Drake are not particularly strong, but Nick has always been a consistent if introverted performer, and placed in the cauldron that Joe Boyd has prepared for him, then things start to effervesce ... it seems nothing has been spared to make this album a success, and Joe Boyd and Nick Drake have certainly succeeded in their intentions.'

In *Melody Maker*, 'AM' was less keen, dismissing the album as 'late night coffee 'n' chat music'. But the general reaction was that Nick might finally have turned the corner. Cat Stevens, Al Stewart, James Taylor and others were carving out a market for sensitive singer-songwriters and Nick was on the verge of fitting into that popular niche. If only he would do some promotion himself. But no. At Island Records, A&R manager Muff Winwood was tearing his hair out: 'Chris Blackwell loved him and was always talking about what a great talent he was, but the rest of us would have given him the boot.' He was even offered an audition for a spot on the forerunner of BBC TV's famous rock show *The Old Grey Whistle Test*, the bizarrely named *Disco 2*, but he failed to turn up. After persistent nagging from Joe Boyd and Anthea

Joseph he did agree to an interview with Jerry Gilbert for *Sounds*, but that was even more of a disaster.

Armed only with a reporters' notebook and a biro, Jerry turned up at the home of Witchseason's PR consultant Frances van Staden in Swiss Cottage, a mile or so from Nick's flat in Belsize Park. 'It was done very painstakingly,' he recalls, 'because Nick hadn't put himself forward to do interviews before and I think I was probably as reluctant to do it as he was. I'm sure I remember getting there first and waiting, and then him eventually shuffling in late. The interview progressed in a very staccato-like fashion, no continuity, lots of dead bats. I don't suppose it lasted very long. I can't even remember leaving at the same time as him. There wasn't a bad atmosphere, there just wasn't any connection whatsoever. You know, of the thousands of interviews I've done over the years it was the strangest.' Jerry Gilbert was an easy-going, thoughtful and respectful interviewer, nothing like the opinionated music journalists of the late 1970s. He would have been very patient with Nick and given him every chance to say what he thought, but in the end he too ran out of patience. Did he like him? 'Well, what's to like? There was nothing expressive about him, I don't think he made eye contact with me once or with anybody. He was just gazing down and he spoke in a monotone, and it's easy to sit here now and glamorise what happened, but I mean there was nothing to like or dislike about him. He was incredibly well spoken, but he was mumbling, so if you wanted to be uncharitable you could say he was just a spoilt boy with a silver spoon and went around feeling sorry for himself. Horrible thing to say but …'.

The *Sounds* article, headed 'Something Else For Nick?', was the first and last Nick Drake interview ever published. In it the 'shy introverted folk singer' was quoted confirming his dislike of live appearances: 'I think the problem was with the material, which I wrote for records rather than performing. There were only two or three concerts that felt right, and there was something wrong with all the others. I did play Cousins and one or two folk clubs in the north, but the gigs just sort of petered out.' Jerry Gilbert described Nick as 'superb' and his songs on *Bryter Layter* as 'stunning', but the interviewee himself wasn't sure. 'I'm not altogether clear about the album – I haven't got to terms with the whole presentation.' Plainly disenchanted with both the artwork and the over-production of *Bryter Layter*, he dropped a bombshell: 'For the next one I had the idea of just doing something with John Wood, the engineer at Sound Techniques.' Joe Boyd and the people at Island were furious. Nick was meant to be promoting his new album not trashing it. And there was no hope of him resuming live work: 'I don't think that would help,' he said, adding the enigmatic sentence: 'If I could find making music a fairly natural connection with something else then I might move on to something else.'

Even though he had done nothing to promote it, Nick was surprised when the sales figures confirmed that *Bryter Layter* had flopped. Robert Kirby says that 'he took that like being hit in the stomach by Mike Tyson. I think that that really did knock him back a long way. And I think he probably stopped writing for a while as well. It's also at that time when his father was suggesting to him that maybe he should be trying some kind of a job.'[91] It was significant that Nick was back in contact with his parents, whose advice he had shunned for two years. The reason was simple. He had been abandoned by his surrogate father Joe Boyd. 'Nick said he was going to make the next record just by himself and my feeling was "you and John can do that without me, you don't need me for that". The Incredible String Band became scientologists, Sandy Denny refused to make a solo record, I was in disagreements with Fairport about leaving a song off *Full House* that I thought should be on. Everywhere I turned it was like they were no longer listening to me. And the company was in debt … so when I got an offer to go to California I thought that was a good solution for everybody.'[92] So Joe Boyd sold Witchseason to Chris Blackwell, paid off his creditors and set off for a new life at Warner Brothers pictures in Hollywood.

As a result of that contract he had signed in 1968, Nick lost his manager, his publisher, his agent and his record producer in one fell swoop. If there was one moment when his despair turned into clinical depression this was probably it. He left Belsize Park, moved briefly into a very run-down flat in Muswell Hill and then abandoned London altogether and went home to Tanworth-in-Arden, telling his mother Molly that he'd failed in everything he'd ever tried to do. Tanworth resident Ray Crabtree, who hadn't seen Nick for a few years, was shocked by his changed appearance. As he told visitors to the 30th anniversary event in August 2004, his earliest memory of Nick was in the mid-1960s at a church fete in the vicarage garden when the young Marlburian, wearing a sports jacket, was helping his father Rodney run the hoop-la stall. 'He was very sprightly, charming, with an athletic build, a picture of health.' Ten years on Ray Crabtree was shocked to see this 'reclusive' figure shuffling along Bates Lane, 'a fugitive hiding inside a long dark blue overcoat. He barely acknowledged us, he wanted to escape from us.' For the last three years of his life, Nick struggled with the search for what he had called A Place To Be. He was restless, both physically and mentally. As he told his mother, 'I don't like it at home, but I can't bear it anywhere else.' And he was still wrestling with the question of whether 'to be or not be'.

His parents did persuade him to seek medical advice for his depression and he was taken to see a psychiatrist at St Thomas's Hospital in London. But Nick was suspicious. His mother Molly told Gorm Henrik Rasmussen that 'something went wrong between us – it never really worked'. Nick knew enough about drugs to worry about the side-effects of some of the pills he was prescribed, especially as he was continuing to smoke cannabis and take occasional hits of heroin. He would refuse his medication, preferring to sit silently in a chair gazing at the wall or out of a window, or simply at his feet. Rodney tried to persuade his only son to snap out of it, have a haircut and get a sensible job, but even he came to realise that Nick was slipping beyond reach.

With any kind of mental illness the development is rarely linear. Unlike physical illnesses, where the patient typically develops symptoms, and then either gets worse and dies or gets treatment and recovers, mental conditions often improve and then worsen again. There are frequent false dawns and periods of progress and optimism that can be dashed by a swift reversal. Gabrielle Drake has described how her parents reacted to Nick's illness: 'a good day for Nick was a good day for them'.[93] No one quite knew what tomorrow would bring.

Occasionally Nick would be energised by a call from a friend or colleague. One day Paul Wheeler invited him to visit the grand mansion in Ascot where his wife was working as a personal assistant. This turned out to be Titenhurst Park, home of John Lennon and Yoko Ono. Whether Nick took a turn on the famous white piano isn't recorded. Another old friend, Robert Kirby, invited him to play guitar on a recording session he was organising for his girlfriend who worked at Longman, the educational publishers. Interplay One was an educational kit for use in secondary schools with poems, stories, film strips and music. Nick played a bass line for I Wish I Was A Single Girl Again, and acoustic rhythm guitar on the sea shanty Full Fathom Five and the old Victorian Australian song With My Swag All On My Shoulder, on which Robert Kirby sang lead vocal. There is no mention of Nick on the sleeve, but the crisp, strong playing is undoubtedly his.[94] Robert Kirby has described Nick's work on the session as 'very professional'.

During the summer of 1971, Chris Blackwell offered Nick

the use of his villa in Algeciras, on Spain's Costa del Sol, to help him recuperate from what Island Records still hoped was a temporary problem. With Joe Boyd in Hollywood and Witchseason sold to Island, Nick was now signed directly to the label, which had taken over paying his weekly retainer. '*Five Leaves Left* was faultless,' says Blackwell today, 'but *Bryter Layter* I didn't like as much – the production was too busy. We were all about giving artists maximum freedom to develop at their own pace so we wanted Nick to take as much time and space as he needed to come up with his next album.' On his way to Spain, travelling alone, Nick stopped off in Paris to call on Françoise Hardy, whom he'd seen briefly while she was recording her English-language album with Tony Cox in London. Nick told John Martyn afterwards that when he'd rung her doorbell and discovered that she was out he couldn't find the courage to leave a message with her maid so he'd simply left without speaking.

* * *

NICK HAD kept in close touch with John Wood, the engineer at Sound Techniques, who had done more than anyone to create the Nick Drake sound. Out of the blue in October 1971, John took a phone call at his home in Mildenhall, Suffolk. It was Nick in Tanworth saying he wanted to make a new record. John knew he had to move quickly, but Sound Techniques was booked solid and the only time he could get in was after the daytime sessions had finished. On his way to the studio,

Nick called at Sophia Ryde's flat, which had many post-impressionist paintings on its walls, and asked her type up the lyrics he'd written in an exercise book. She wasn't at all happy with the words to a song called Free Ride, which referred to 'the pictures that you hang on the wall' and seemed to be a play on her surname and a none too subtle plea for her to be more understanding. 'We went in one night,' John Wood told BBC Radio 2, 'put up four microphones, probably did five or six songs straight off and Nick was very quiet throughout.' Linda Thompson, who visited the studio that night, agrees that Nick didn't speak. 'He was in a dreadful state, totally incommunicado. I'm surprised he didn't throw me out. He didn't speak to John Wood either.' Woody asked if he wanted to record more songs the following evening. 'I just assumed at some point he was going to say "Well I want to get hold of Robert." So I turned round at the end of the second evening and said, "Well what do you think? What do you want to put on?" And he said, "I don't want anything on." And I said, "Absolutely nothing?" And he said, "No that's all I want." And we just mixed it, very quickly, Nick went off with the tapes to Island Records and that was *Pink Moon*.'

There was in fact one overdub on Nick's third album, a beautiful piano part he added to the title track. Otherwise, the album was 28 minutes of bleak solo acoustic guitar and vocals. As he'd predicted in his interview with Jerry Gilbert, Nick had made a simple, spare record, uncluttered by anyone else's arrangements or instrumentation. John Wood has described it as 'a reaction to the rather shimmering production of *Bryter Layter'*, but it was more than that. *Pink Moon* was the only record Nick could have made at the time. Apart from two more complex songs, Parasite and Things Behind The Sun, which dated from earlier times,[95] this was a collection of songs from the edge. There was no room for artifice, for showbusiness polish or rock star shtick. Nick was coming apart and *Pink Moon* was the journal of his experience. Know has just four lines, ending in the despairing 'I see you ... I'm not there'. Harvest Breed has him 'falling fast and falling free', looking to find a friend. In Road, Nick will 'take a road that'll see me through'. *Pink Moon* itself picks up the theme of foreboding. Fishermen say that when the moon is surrounded by a pink haze, something bad is going to happen. In Nick's case, the pink moon, which is 'gonna get ye all', is almost certainly a metaphor for death.

What happened next is regularly misrepresented in biographies of Nick Drake. The traditional story is that Nick turned up at Island's Basing Street office, left the tape of *Pink Moon* in reception and slunk away unrecognised. The truth is that he did go to Island with a quarter-inch stereo mix of the album, but when he arrived he asked if he could see Chris Blackwell. 'I got a call from reception that a Nick Drake was here to see me,' recalls Blackwell, 'so I went downstairs. He was very uncommunicative, very introverted – "Hi Nick how are you?", "Oh fine, here's my new record." I asked him what it had cost and he said 500 or so pounds so I gave him the money there and then. It was hard to put pressure on someone who wouldn't tour when their record only cost 500 quid!'

10. Black Eyed Dog

AS SOON AS *Pink Moon* arrived at Island Records, Keith Morris was booked for a new photo shoot on Hampstead Heath, not far from Nick's old flat in Belsize Park. He and Nick had kept in touch since the *Bryter Layter* session, mainly because Nick would turn up unannounced at the flat Keith shared with his girlfriend Kathy. 'He'd pop in for a cuppa, wouldn't say much, then he'd just get up and say "I must be going now." You'd think "Well that was strange."' Annie Sullivan from Island's press office arrived in a limousine to pick up Keith and his cameras, and Nick was already sitting in the back of the car. 'I talked to myself for an hour,' recalls Keith. 'He wasn't unhelpful, he occasionally smiled in a shy kind of way but it was a bit sad how much he'd changed.' It was a bleak and grey day, which matched Nick's mood, and the session lasted less than an hour. The first location was an alleyway between numbers 94 and 96 South Hill Park in Hampstead. A few yards further on Keith sat Nick on a park bench, which has now been removed, overlooking one of the Hampstead Ponds. His hunched figure and blank expression told their own story.

Island decided against using Keith Morris's shots for the album sleeve and instead wrapped *Pink Moon* in a curious Dali-esque painting by Gabrielle Drake's friend Michael Trevithick. Knowing that Nick wouldn't tour, record any radio or TV sessions or even agree to be interviewed, the label's press officer, David Sandison, took the unusual step of spending the entire promotional budget on a full-page advert in the UK music papers. Alongside the South Park Hill photograph, with Nick walking away from the camera and Annie Sullivan's golden retriever Gus yapping at his feet, Sandison dashed off a passionate and highly personal plea for readers to buy Nick's new album. It is a fascinating insight into how the Nick Drake story was seen at the time:

PINK MOON – NICK DRAKE'S NEW ALBUM:
THE FIRST WE HEARD OF IT WAS WHEN IT WAS
FINISHED.

The first time I ever heard Nick Drake was when I joined Island and picked out his first album 'Five Leaves Left' from the shelf and decided to listen to it because the cover looked good.

From the opening notes of Time Has Told Me to the last chord of Saturday Sun, I was held by the totally personal feel of the music, the words and by that strange feeling you get when you accidentally intrude on someone else's phone conversation.

The first time I ever saw Nick Drake was at the Queen Elizabeth Hall. He came on with his guitar, sat on a stool, looked at the floor and sang a series of muffled songs punctuated by mumbled thanks for the scattering of bewildered applause from the audience who didn't know who the hell he was, nor cared too much. At the end of his last song, his guitar still holding the final notes of the song, he got up and walked off; his shoulders hunched as if to protect him from actually having to meet people.

The first time I ever met Nick Drake was the week his 2nd album 'Bryter Layter' was released. He arrived an hour late, wasn't very interested in a cup of coffee or tea or anything to eat. During the next half hour he said maybe two words. Eventually I ran out of voice, paid the bill and walked him back to Witchseason.

The last time I saw Nick was a week or so ago. He came in, smiling that weird smile of his and handed over his new album. He'd just gone into the studios and recorded it without telling a soul except the engineer. And we haven't seen him since.

The point of this story is this: why (when there are people prepared to do almost anything for a recording contract or a Queen Elizabeth Hall date) are we releasing this new Nick Drake Album, and (if he wants to make one) – the next?

Because, quite simply we believe that Nick Drake is a great talent. His first two albums haven't sold a shit. But, if we carry on releasing them, then maybe one day someone authoritative will stop, listen properly

*and agree with us. Then maybe a lot more people will
get to hear Nick Drake's incredible songs and guitar
playing. And maybe they'll buy a lot of his albums, and
fulfill* [sic] *our faith in Nick's promise.*

   Then. Then we'll have done our job.
   Dave Sandison – December 1971

On February 25, 1972, *Pink Moon* was released into a
British market suffering from rota'd power cuts and the three-
day working week as a result of the government's response to
a miners' strike. Railways, the post, transport and distribution
services were all badly affected and newspapers were putting
out emergency editions. Once again the marketing of a Nick
Drake album seemed fated. The first review of *Pink Moon*
wasn't published until a month after its release. In it Jerry
Gilbert, possibly still smarting from the experience of
interviewing Nick, told *Sounds* readers that 'the songs are not
sufficiently strong to stand up without any embroidery at all
... maybe it's time Mr. Drake stopped acting so mysteriously
and started getting something properly organised for himself.'
Melody Maker didn't review the album until May 1st, when
Mark Plummer wrote 'John Martyn told me about Nick Drake
in ecstatic terms and so it seemed the natural thing to do, bag
the album when it came in, for review that is. It is hard to say
whether John was right or not. His music is so personal and
shyly presented both lyrically and in his confined guitar and
piano playing that it neither does or doesn't come over ... The
more you listen to Drake though, the more compelling his

music becomes – but all the time it hides from you.' In a prophetic postscript he added, 'It could be that Nick Drake does not exist at all.'

In a way Nick didn't exist any more. The old Nick, the ambitious Nick, the driven Nick, had been replaced by a sullen and pathetic figure who seemed increasingly detached from the world. There were moments of lucidity and times of apparent improvement in his condition, but during the next two years he slipped gradually into a vortex of despair. He was living at home in his old bedroom at Far Leys attended by his parents and by Naw, the Karen maid. Naw told her friend Easter that, winter or summer, she would look for Nick's overcoat on its peg. If it was there, he was in. If it wasn't, he was gone, sometimes for days at a time, without ever telling his family where he was going. Often he would borrow Molly's car and drive aimlessly until he ran out of petrol. Sometimes he would seek out a drug dealer and take a hit away from his parents' censure. Occasionally he would seek out old friends, always turning up unannounced and usually shocking them with his withdrawn behaviour and his dishevelled appearance.

Robert Kirby described a typical visit: 'He would arrive and not talk, sit down, listen to music, have a smoke, have a drink, possibly go to the pub, sleep there the night, and two or three days later you'd turn around and he wasn't there, he'd gone. And three months later he'd be back. With hindsight I feel I should have done something, but at the time you thought, "Well, he's a great artist in creative mode."'

Nick would sometimes visit John Wood and his family in Mildenhall, Suffolk. 'Nobody nagged him, he used to sit around with the kids, my wife Sheila and I, and nobody ever bothered him. He didn't really look after himself personally very well. His clothes would be a mess and things like that. But, I don't know, for some reason one felt it was better to let him be as he was than to try and intrude.'[96] Nick also made regular visits to the south coast of England, to John and Beverley Martyn's house in Hastings, and to nearby Eastbourne where he would stay with Marian, the wife of his Cambridge friend Brian Wells, and her parents. 'He would always leave without saying goodbye,' recalls Brian. Sometimes he couldn't even find the courage to knock on the door. Beverley Martyn told Peter Paphides of the *Observer* about an occasion when a neighbour called to say, 'Oh, Nick Drake's on the beach, shall I go down and get him?' He'd been 'just staring out into space, in a dark suit while everyone else was in their swimming costumes'.

Beverley Martyn had become one of Nick's closest confidantes. 'He would just come and spend the day or the night. I would make up a bed for him, maybe we'd take the dog for a walk. There wouldn't be a lot of words said. Sometimes, he'd play me things. We even wrote a little song together, Reckless Jane. I think I put most of the words to it, but it was never finished. You just had to let him do what he wanted really, which was either play the same album over and over again, or look out the window with a cup of tea in his hands for four hours.' John Martyn's exasperation with his old friend resulted in his famous song Solid Air, released in 1973: 'I don't know what's going on in your mind, but I know you don't like what you find, when you're moving through solid air.' At the time Martyn said, 'it was done for a friend of mine and it was done with very clear motives and I'm very pleased with it'. Paul Wheeler remembers Martyn phoning him when he'd finished it. 'He sang it down the phone with no accompaniment. That was typical of John, no division between his life and work.'

Paul Wheeler sensed that Nick knew he was damaged. 'What was going on in his head was something uncontrollable. He complained about everything going out of his hands, that he was controlled by powers beyond his reach – the record company, the business men ... the whole system.'[97] Brian Wells also had visits at his Chilton Street flat in London. 'He would turn up in this old car and stay round for an hour and then he would leave and I'd get a phone call from his dad saying "Nick's just phoned and he's run out of petrol" or "he hasn't put any oil in his car and the engine's seized, can you go and find him".' John Venning, Nick's supervision partner at Cambridge, was staying in London when he saw Nick on a tube train. 'I suddenly became aware that the person propping up the wall opposite me was Nick. I was moved to go and talk to him, but as I got nearer I thought "there's something incredibly wrong here" ... I thought he was really seriously clinically depressed. There was something about him which suggested that he would have looked straight through me and not registered me at all. So I turned round.'

Brian Wells hadn't seen Nick for over a year when the phone rang. 'It was Rodney, Nick's dad. He said, "Nick's really not very well but he doesn't want people to know."' Rodney suggested that Nick might benefit from a visit by his old friend. 'So I just started to show up at their house in Tanworth-in-Arden and we'd kind of get on for a bit and then it would become awkward and he'd become withdrawn.' At first, Wells, now one of the country's leading psychiatrists, whose speciality is addiction, didn't think Nick was mentally ill. 'I thought it was just an extreme version of what I'd seen at Cambridge, where he was self-conscious, image conscious, aloof, slightly arrogant, with his dad's sense of humour, very dry, quite condescending. One day we played *Bryter Layter* all the way through and I said, "Well if I'd made a record like that and it hadn't sold I'd have been in the pits", and he said, "Yeh, now you see."'

Another old friend summoned by Nick's family was John Martyn. In an interview recorded by BBC producer Dave Barber in 1991 but not aired until 2004, he recalled walking round the garden with Nick at Far Leys. 'He was really, really withdrawn, he found it difficult to speak. And I said, "Listen, what the hell's gone wrong with you? Did you think you were going to be a star overnight?" And he said, "Yes, I fucking did." And I said, "Well, what's the problem there? You're not. Sit down, make some more music and you will be. I mean, don't worry, you're beautiful and you're great." And he just proceeded to enter into a tirade about the injustices of the world.'

On other occasions the old Nick briefly re-emerged. Brian Wells remembers a surreal afternoon in the music room on the ground floor of Far Leys when Nick grabbed his old saxophone and started belting out Duane Eddy's Theme From Peter Gunn while Brian tried to keep up on the guitar. Another day, Nick painstakingly showed Brian how to play his song From The Morning using his CGCFCF tuning. But the good days were few and far between. At his local doctor's suggestion, Nick was admitted for observation to a local psychiatric hospital, Barnsley Hall in Bromsgrove. Brian Wells recalls calling him there from Far Leys. 'I said, "I'm at your mum and dad's house do you mind if I come and see you?", and he said, "This isn't a nut house you know, I'm not in a nut house", which of course it was, and that was where his psychiatrist started him on Tryptizol.' From then on Nick's behaviour was controlled by prescription drugs. When they worked he appeared almost normal. When they didn't, he suffered massive mood swings.

* * *

BY 1974, the weekly retainer from Island had dried up. Hearing that Joe Boyd, still his manager, agent and publisher, was back in the UK on a fleeting visit, Nick decided to visit him. 'He looked terrible,' Joe Boyd told the BBC. 'His hair was dirty and he was unshaven and his fingernails were dirty and he was wearing a shabby coat. He wasn't the sort of diffident shy person I had remembered. He was very agitated, very nervous, twitchy. He sat down and he immediately launched into this kind of tirade about his career, about money and basically it was accusatory. And he said, "You told me I'm great, but nobody knows me. Nobody buys my records. I'm still living on handouts from the publishing company. I don't understand. What's wrong? Whose fault is this?" And he was angry. And I tried to explain that there's no guarantees, that you can make a great record and sometimes it just doesn't sell.'

The only answer seemed to be to make another record, so Nick called John Wood again and booked a session at Sound Techniques. The result was the harrowing Black Eyed Dog, as disturbing a piece of music as Mahler's Ninth Symphony or Hellhound On My Trail by the tormented blues guitarist Robert Johnson. From the depths of Sound Techniques' eerie echo room,[98] Nick's guitar rang like a funeral bell. From the depths of his own tortured soul, his fractured voice cried out 'I'm growin' old and I wanna go home.'

'He had no interest in living at all,' remembers Linda Thompson. 'The fruits of life meant nothing – shopping, sex, laughter – I don't remember him ever laughing.' She too was shocked by his appearance. 'Just before he died he looked like Howard Hughes. There was this beautiful boy with the milky white, almost see-through skin, who always took great care of his hands and his fingernails, and now he was dirty and unkempt and his nails were too long to play the guitar.'

His old friend from Marlborough and Aix, Simon Crocker, had lost touch with Nick when he bumped into 'someone who said Nick's in a bad way. I wrote a letter to him care of Island

Records saying "Nick I'm in London if you're around give me a ring", and about five weeks later the phone rang and it was Nick saying "Hi, how are you, yeh, I'd love to come and see you", so I gave him the address in Chelsea Square and Nick found his way there and it was heartbreaking because there was someone I'd known as laid-back but relaxed and smiley, and he could hardly put two words together and I don't know how he'd made his way across London. And I sat there kind of reaching out but he was incoherent. I knew he was in really bad shape and I said, "Look Nick is there anything I can do?", and he said, "Well no I don't think so", and I said, "Well just ring me if there's anything I can do." And then he kind of disappeared after about an hour. I never saw him again.'

Roddy Llewellyn, who was by then involved in his affair with Princess Margaret, saw Nick one day in 1974 when they were both driving round Marble Arch in London. The sight of the formerly bright and handsome student from Aix made an indelible impression on him. 'I saw him through the car window and I waved, but he was looking very perturbed, his face was filled with angst. I can see him really clearly even now, it's a picture I'll never forget.'

Nick was particularly distressed by two suicides in 1974. On May 7th, the organist Graham Bond threw himself in front of a train at Finsbury Park station, close to the Manor House pub where Nick had seen him play in 1966. Soon afterwards, Julian Ormsby-Gore, the filmmaker and brother of Nick's friend Victoria Lloyd, shot himself.

In July 1974, however, there seemed to be an improvement. Nick called John Wood again and announced that he was ready to finish his fourth album. By his own recent standards, he sounded enthusiastic and motivated, but the sessions were as uncomfortable as before. Joe Boyd was horrified to see the deterioration in Nick's performance: 'He couldn't even sing and play the guitar at the same time.' Compared to the confident, note-perfect recordings of 1968 and 1969, it was a tragic spectacle, 'listening to him try to play just a guitar track and making mistakes and stopping and going back to the beginning and apologising ... and then coming back the next day, putting on headphones, listening to his guitar and singing very hesitantly with mistakes over his own guitar.' The new songs were a disappointment too. Voice From A Mountain[99] dated back to the 1969 'work tape' and had been overlooked in favour of better material in the meantime. The other songs showed that the poetry in Nick's lyrics had been replaced by paranoia and bitterness. 'Why leave me hanging on a star when you deem me so high?', he wailed at Joe Boyd. Rider On The Wheel was pleasant enough, and the mis-spelt Tow The Line,[100] which didn't emerge on record until 2004, had a strong melody line, but neither suggested that Nick's muse had returned or that he had it in him to make a hit album. They would be the last tracks he ever recorded.

Shortly afterwards he managed to get himself to Paris, where some of his Chelsea friends had rented a houseboat. He may even have hooked up again briefly with Françoise Hardy, who told Patrick Humphries that she has a clear recollection of dining with Nick, although he said not one word to her all evening. But on his return to Tanworth his parents and his sister sensed he was past his worst and that the corner might have been turned. He even agreed to get a regular job. Rodney Drake found a company that would take him on to work with computers, but as his mother Molly told the BBC, 'he passed a few tests, much to our amazement really, but then they sent him straight off down to some place where he was entirely alone on a course and he just chucked it and thought, "Well this is absurd, I should be going back to music."' Bizarrely, Molly also remembered Nick deciding to join the Army. 'That was a pretty good disaster. He went for the interview, but he didn't even bother to have his hair cut – it was down to his shoulders.'

Paul Wheeler's recollection of his final meeting with Nick is especially poignant. 'I remember him turning up wearing glasses and with his hair cut, and me thinking that these were symbols of having given in to the Establishment! We were in my car, and Nick asked my advice about what to do with depression – he seemed to think that I had more experience of getting in and out of it. I looked at him with surprise, assuming that he had more answers than me; the result was that I think we both had a chill of feeling stranded – both having assumed that the other had "the map".'

When his illness allowed, Nick had been trying to sustain his relationship with Sophia Ryde. He would never invite her to Far Leys, but he often turned up at her London flat, where she recalls his embarrassment at having to take his medication.

'He would be staying at my flat and we would be talking, and he'd say "Do you mind if I go into the kitchen and take my pills? I'm frightfully sorry, frightfully sorry."' On the afternoon of November 24, 1974, Nick sat in his room at Far Leys and began a letter to Sophia, which he folded carefully and put in a sealed envelope by his bed. Thirty years on she admits that he was heartbroken when she called a halt to their on-off relationship at about this time. 'I couldn't cope with it,' she recalls. 'I asked him for some time. I never saw him again.'

That Saturday evening Nick went to bed early. He took his pills, smoked some cigarettes and listened to music from Bach's Brandenburg Concertos, the record he had bought during those happy months in Aix seven years earlier. He lay down and tried to sleep, but at about six in the morning he got up and went to the kitchen where he ate a bowl of cornflakes in cold milk. He went back to his bedroom and took some more pills. Too many pills. He picked up a copy of *The Myth Of Sisyphus*, a collection of essays by the French philosopher Albert Camus, which begins: 'There is but one serious philosophical problem and that is suicide. Judging whether life is or is not worth living amounts to answering the fundamental question of philosophy.'

At noon on November 25, 1974, Molly Drake opened the door of her only son's bedroom to find him lying across his single bed dressed only in his underpants. His 26-year-old heart had stopped beating. The life of Nick Drake had ended. The legend was about to begin.

4. Now We Rise and We Are Everywhere

11. Aftermath

MOLLY DRAKE was inconsolable, the shock of her son's death made more unbearable by the appalling circumstances of her discovery of his body. Looking at the bottle of orange Tryptizol capsules by his bedside, she calculated that he had taken about 30 since the previous evening. In a frenzy of grief, she and Rodney called their family doctor and tidied Nick's room. There was no suicide note, but on his desk they found the letter addressed to Sophia Ryde and an exercise book containing the lyrics to all his songs, written in his familiar sloping longhand. There were no crossings-out or alterations: it looked like Nick's last testament.

The Drakes decided against phoning Nick's actress sister Gabrielle, who was in Bristol preparing for an opening night, and instead sent her a telegram stating that they would be making a surprise visit on the following day. Rodney travelled to Birmingham to place an announcement in the 'Deaths' column of the local paper:

DRAKE – on November 25 Nicholas Rodney (Nick)

*aged 26 years, beloved son of Rodney & Molly, dearest
brother of Gabrielle. Funeral service Tanworth-in-Arden
Church on Monday December 2 at 12.15 p.m. No
flowers please.*

When her parents told her what had happened Gabrielle
wasn't surprised. She had sensed that her brother had had
enough and she took some comfort from the fact that his
suffering was over. Many people who knew Nick felt the same.
Joe Boyd was back in America: 'I was shocked and I was very
sad, but it's not like somebody is in the best of health and
everything is fine and all of a sudden you hear they dropped
dead.' John Wood told the BBC, 'I never expected it, but …
there'd be other people who would have surprised me much
more.' Brian Wells felt 'sad but not altogether surprised'.
Robert Kirby said 'he was ready for death all right, I just think
he'd had enough, there was no fight left in him'. Ashley
Hutchings, who had first discovered Nick, remembers that
the music business 'knew he was in a bad way'. At Island
Records there was resignation. Muff Winwood, Head of A&R,
recalls 'we saw it coming, we just shrugged our shoulders and
thought well, that wasn't unexpected'.

Most of the music papers noted Nick's death with a small
paragraph, but at *Sounds* Jerry Gilbert wrote a 600-word article
headlined 'Nick Drake – Death Of A Genius', published on
December 14th. In it, he described Nick's 'legacy of three superb,
stylised albums' and explained that he 'had been ill – perhaps
weary is a better expression – for some time'. It was Robert

Kirby who was quoted as saying 'he was a genius', but Jerry Gilbert's own description was less conclusive. 'Nick Drake was a complete enigma. There was an ominous portent in a lot of his work and … the outside world was something he found difficult to look squarely in the face. He seldom raised his eyes from the ground and would walk around with a curious enigmatic half-smile most of the time.' The article also quoted Robert Kirby saying 'Nick Drake should not be built into a legend or some kind of posthumous superhero in the way that Jim Croce was. He would never have wished for that.'

Speculation about the cause of Nick's death started immediately and has continued feverishly ever since. Was it suicide or an accident? Was it a cry for help or an impetuous decision to make something, anything, happen? Did he know the power of the Tryptizol tablets? What else was he taking that the family doctor didn't know about? Today, in the case of a sudden or unexpected death involving drugs, the answers would be provided by a post-mortem, extensive blood and urine tests, and an inquest. But the 1970s were a less sophisticated time. The half-empty pill bottle was the smoking gun that gave the Drakes and their family doctor all the evidence they needed. The coroner was alerted and a Form E was issued, allowing the body to be released for cremation after the most cursory of medical examinations. An inquest was held by the coroner for the Southern District of Warwickshire, Dr H Stephen Tibbits, more than two weeks after the cremation on December 18th, the only evidence being the family doctor's testimony. On that basis alone a death certificate was issued on December 24th, stating cause of death as 'Acute Amitriptyline Poisoning – self administered when suffering from a depressive illness.' In brackets was added the word 'suicide'. Since Nick's death many people have tried to find suspicious motives in these events. Articles have appeared speculating that the Drake family somehow wanted to keep details of Nick's drug use out of the public eye and even a retired GP told me that the story 'smacks of a cover-up'. But it does look likely that the Drakes were simply guarding their privacy. In the conservative middle-class community of Tanworth-in-Arden, a suicide would have been something to keep well hidden.

What we do know, from Rodney Drake's letter to his friend from Burma, James Lusk,[101] the doctor who had delivered Nick Drake in June 1948, is that his son had been prescribed three drugs: Tryptizol, Stelazine and Disipal. It was like the old lady who swallowed the bird to catch the spider and swallowed the spider to catch the fly ...

Tryptizol, a brand name for amitriptyline, is a tricyclic antidepressant used by doctors to treat depression, anxiety and mood swings. It works by increasing levels of the neurotransmitters serotonin and noradrenaline in the brain. For a while during the 1970s it became fashionable as a tranquilliser or sleeping pill, rather like Valium and Prozac in more recent times. Nick may well have been told that his Tryptizol tablets were simply to help him sleep. Stelazine contains the antipsychotic drug trifluoperazine, which blocks a variety of receptors in the brain, particularly dopamine receptors. Dopamine is involved in transmitting signals between brain cells, and when there is an excess amount of it in the brain it causes over-stimulation of dopamine receptors. These receptors normally act to modify behaviour, and over-stimulating them can cause psychotic illness. Stelazine is designed to decrease anxiety and agitation, but it can cause blurred vision, a dry mouth and insomnia. Disipal, a brand name for orphenadrine, is therefore prescribed to counteract the side effects of the decreased dopamine in the brain, which can resemble early symptoms of Parkinson's disease like abnormal face and body movements, restlessness and tremor, just the behaviour Joe Boyd and John Wood noted when Nick was recording his final session. But it too can cause insomnia, which is where the Tryptizol comes in … It can be a vicious pharmaceutical circle.

Nick may have believed that continuing to smoke cannabis would help him feel better. But he couldn't have been more wrong. In 2003, Professor Robin Murray of the London Institute of Psychiatry told the *Guardian* newspaper that 'people with chronic psychotic illnesses were more likely to be regular daily consumers of cannabis than the general population'. Cannabis, like amphetamine and cocaine, increases the release of dopamine in the brain. Professor Murray said, 'if you're taking cannabis daily by age 18, then you are about seven times more likely to develop schizophrenia than the rest of the population'. A recent Swedish study followed 50,000 people for 15 years from the age of 18. Those who had tried cannabis by 18 were 2.4 times as likely to be diagnosed with schizophrenia than those who had never used it. The risk apparently increased the more cannabis was used. An Australian study reported in the *British Medical Journal* showed that girls who smoked cannabis were five times more likely to suffer from depression. A *British Medical Journal* editorial in 2002 concluded that the link between cannabis and psychosis was 'well established'.

It seems likely therefore that Nick was suffering from a psychosis, probably mild schizophrenia, which was brought on by excessive use of cannabis. The cannabis increased his dopamine, the Stelazine decreased it and the Disipal increased it again. Meanwhile he reached for the Tryptizol to try and get some sleep. But the tricyclic antidepressants are notoriously easy to overdose. If Nick had been prescribed 10mg tablets, he was probably instructed to take ten or more a day; 30 tablets may have been only slightly more than two doses. But that amount can be lethal, causing death through a failure of the muscles of the heart, usually between two and four hours after the drug has been consumed.

It is customary to show intent when registering a suicide and in the absence of a note, the mere presence of a half-empty bottle of pills and a copy of Albert Camus' book about suicide was anything but cast-iron proof. Dr Brian Wells for one disputes the voracity of the inquest verdict. 'I don't think he committed suicide. It was a kind of "what the hell". It was hard for the coroner to say anything but suicide, but I think if Nick had wanted to die he'd have taken aspirin or jumped under a train or something, or hanged himself.'[102] Brian Wells

A fully psychedelicised Nick, clad in a hippy blanket, proudly displaying his harvest of magic mushrooms in a Welsh forest probably 1970.

Singer Linda Thompson (neé Peters), close friend of Nick's, later married to guitarist Richard Thompson.

The old Chelsea dairy at 46a Old Church St, London SW3, site of Sound Techniques studio where Nick recorded his three albums.

The site of Joe Boyd's Witchseason office, 83 Charlotte St, London, W1.

Nick in the window of his Belsize Park garden flat at 112 Haverstock Hill, London, June 1970.

Sucking on the ever-present joint, Nick ambles along a beach near Harlech Castle Wales with his familiar stoop and bowed head, probably 1970.

Nick stares vacantly at photographer Keith Morris during their final photo shoot near Hampstead Ponds. 'It was like intruding on private grief wrote Morris, 'previously we'd made pictures together, on this occasion I recorded him.' November 1971.

The site of Nick's ground floor flat on Haverstock Hill, Belsize Park London. The old Victorian building was pulled down in the 1980s but would have looked like the two houses to its left.

THE SESQUIALTERA STOP WAS GIVEN
IN MEMORY OF
NICHOLAS DRAKE
AND HIS MUSIC
BY HIS FAMILY IN 1977

The Tanworth church organ and its plaque recording the installation of a new stop in Nick's memory.

The graveyard of the church of St Mary Magdalene, Tanworth-in-Arden. Nick's grave under an oak tree overlooking the Warwickshire countryside.

Nick's gravestone, Tanworth-in-Arden. The inscription on the rear comes from Nick's song From The Morning.

Nick with Gus on South Park Hill, Hampstead, Autumn 1971. Part of his final shoot with Keith Morris, this is the shot used by Island records for the despairing full-page ad written by David Sandison.

is also critical of the diagnosis by Nick's family doctor and by the psychiatric hospital he attended. 'I didn't think he was depressed in a way that was going to respond to psychotropic drugs. He wasn't like Peter Green or Syd Barrett, where the chemicals precipitated an underlying schizophrenic tendency. I did get a sense of low self-esteem – "I am a parasite who clings to your skirt" – I certainly didn't get a sense of depressive illness with suicidal intent.'

However Gabrielle Drake has often said that she does believe that Nick wanted to end his life. In 2004 she told Belgian Radio that her parents were 'terribly distressed that the coroner thought it was suicide. For myself I prefer to think that he meant to take his own life than that it was a terrible accident. While I don't think it was premeditated on a conscious level, I think in a way it's underestimating Nick to think that somewhere he didn't really mean to end his life. I think somewhere deep down it was a decision he made.'

* * *

THE FUNERAL was conducted by Canon E Willmott at the Church of St Mary Magdalene in Tanworth-in-Arden, where Nick had sung many times in the choir. There were about 50 mourners, drawn from all the different compartments of Nick's life. The Chelsea set, the music business people from Island and Witchseason, old friends from Cambridge, Aix, Marlborough and Tanworth met each other for the first time. Rodney Drake described how 'a lot of his young friends came up here. We'd never met many of them. They were wonderful people and they all said that it really wasn't anything to do with [us] – we were just the same, we could never get through to him either.'[103] After a procession by road to Solihull Crematorium, seven miles away, the party returned to Far Leys for a wake. It was a miserable affair. The usual funeral platitudes about a good innings didn't apply and neither could anyone who knew him really say that Nick would be sadly missed or that a promising young life had been snuffed out. Sure, his death was a tragedy, but it was a also a relief to everyone who knew and loved him and had witnessed his decline. There were no commemorative compilation albums, no Sunday-paper obituaries, no TV documentaries. After his ashes were interred under a large oak tree in Tanworth graveyard on January 14, 1975, Nick's only other memorial would be his three largely unknown albums.

For a decade, that's where the Nick Drake story ended. In 1975 Richard and Linda Thompson released a song on their *Pour Down Like Silver* album called Poor Boy Is Taken Away, which included the lines 'called him poor boy, you took him for fun, he dressed for the tinkering trade, now the poor boy is taken away'. Linda Thompson has no memory of recording the song, but it seems likely that she and Nick were the subjects of the third verse: 'no use standing, waving adieu … the old flame has left you behind'. And there were occasional references to Nick in the music papers, including an impassioned piece by Nick Kent in the *New Musical Express* disputing the suicide verdict, and a lengthy memoir by Island's David Sandison in

Zig Zag. But during the punk and post-punk years, Nick Drake's gentle acoustic music was largely ignored. Oddly, though, I always had a feeling that if properly promoted, his music could reach a broader audience. While presenting shows on BBC Radio Nottingham in the 1970s, I would occasionally slip in a Nick Drake track. There was always a positive reaction, sometimes from listeners, sometimes just from other workers on the radio station. Unknown and unrecognised he may have been in his lifetime, but that plaintive, mournful sound always seemed to strike a chord with people, who would ask who he was and what had happened to him. I imagined I was alone in making literally dozens of cassette tapes for people to help them get into Nick's music, but it turned out there were lots of people doing the same thing all over the world.

Island Records remained unmoved until 1979. Five years earlier it had categorically denied any 'intention of re-packaging Nick's recordings, either now or at any time in the foreseeable future'. Referring to Nick's 1974 recordings, Island's press officer Richard Williams, now a very distinguished sports journalist, added that 'Nick himself expressed dissatisfaction with the four songs he recorded late last year, consequently John Wood has destroyed the 16-track master tapes – with our full approval.' But four years after Nick's death it was decided to package his three albums plus the four then unreleased tracks into a boxed set called *The Complete Collected Works*, retailing at £9.50, a huge sum in those inflation-ridden days. Nick Kent was commissioned to write the sleeve notes and delivered a brilliant, if somewhat verbose, essay commending Nick's 'shimmering sensuousness and brooding mellifluousness' and describing his music as 'irrepressibly beguiling in its distant seductiveness'.[104] But Island decided that the tone of Kent's work wasn't celebratory enough, and asked a passing American journalist Arthur Lubow, now best known as a food writer for the *New York Times*, to write some notes instead. Lubow name-checked Tom Verlaine of the American art-punk band Television as a Drake fan and quoted the music business giant David Geffen saying, 'I thought Nick Drake should have been a star and I could help him. I kept asking Island about him and they kept putting me off. And then it was too late.' Nick's name was starting to appear in exalted company. Every writer since Lubow owes him a great debt for the research he did in 1978 for the boxed set that finally emerged as *Fruit Tree*.[105]

Not unexpectedly *Fruit Tree* did little to popularise Nick's music. It was too expensive for the casual consumer and packaged in a drab navy-blue cover with no photographs. Once again the marketing of Nick's music had let it down. For the next few years, Nick's memory was sustained by his parents, who had come to love and cherish their son's music much more than they had during his lifetime. They were genuinely surprised and flattered by the attention that he received from young visitors and they showed remarkable patience with the pilgrims, many of them American, who would make the journey to Far Leys. Nick's room had been kept as it was when he died and young fans would often be shown up and even allowed to photograph it. Molly would direct them to the parish church where they could sign the visitors' book and see the special stop designed to add sparkle and brilliance to the organ's tone. The plaque reads: 'The sesquialtera stop was given in memory of Nicholas Drake and his music by his family 1977'. Rodney would even run off tapes of Nick's home recordings and hand them out with copies of Nick's notes and papers. Sadly a great deal of potentially valuable memorabilia disappeared during this time.

The real turning point in Nick's profile came in the mid-1980s. Robert Smith of The Cure credited the lyrics of Time Has Told Me ('a troubled cure for a troubled mind') with the inspiration for his band's name. Peter Buck and Michael Stipe of REM dropped Nick's name in interviews, and recruited Joe Boyd to produce their album *Fables Of The Reconstruction*. Then an English trio called The Dream Academy – Nick Laird-Clowes, Gilbert Gabriel and Kate St John – made the UK and US charts in 1985 with Life In A Northern Town, co-produced by Pink Floyd's Dave Gilmour. The breathy vocals of Laird-Clowes (often referred to as 'Loud Clothes') were not unlike Nick's and the picture sleeve contained a dedication to 'Nick Drake, Steve Reich & Classics For Pleasure'. Laird-Clowes told the *Melody Maker* that the song 'has a strong connection with Nick Drake in a way I can't even explain'. Perhaps it was a subconscious echo of Nick's Northern Sky. Either way, Mike Read, then presenting the breakfast show on BBC Radio 1, played the Dream Academy single, mentioned the dedication and started to get requests for Nick Drake music.

Listening to the station at the time was Island's new head of A&R, Nick Stewart, the same Nick Stewart who had known Nick Drake all those years ago at Eagle House prep school. Sensing that Nick Drake's music was perfect for the adult compact disc market that was just emerging, Stewart persuaded Island to release a single-album 'best of' compilation. On a visit to Los Angeles to film a segment for the BBC TV show *Whistle Test*, which I was producing, Stewart and I reminisced about Nick Drake, and when we got home he rang and asked me to compile the album. It was a huge honour. Down came the old vinyl albums, in went the cassette and off to Island went a running order that started with Fruit Tree, ended with Time Has Told Me and included four more tracks from *Five Leaves Left*, four from *Bryter Layter* and three from *Pink Moon*. Joe Boyd was consulted about my list and insisted, quite rightly, that Northern Sky should replace Three Hours. I can't believe I left it off. And where is my other favourite Fly? And Black Eyed Dog? Anyway, we were all happy at the time. Nick Stewart was especially proud of the title: 'Heaven In A Wild Flower' was a quotation from the poet William Blake, a favourite of Nick Drake's. The only problem was marketing. The Nick Drake album jinx struck again when Nick Stewart showed Island MD Dave Robinson the two-tone dummy for the sleeve. 'It was the worst cover of all time,' says Nick Stewart, 'but Robbo liked the mock-up and he said, "Well let's just go with that."' At last, however, Nick had a hit on his hands. *Heaven In A Wild Flower* sold in excess of 20,000 copies in the UK, twice as many as the total sales of the first three albums and the boxed set put together.

Also in 1985, Joe Boyd happened upon the original master tapes of Nick's Sound Techniques sessions, which had been stored in Island's chaotic library. The *Fruit Tree* box had been deleted in 1983, but Joe negotiated a deal to release an enhanced version on his own Hannibal label. On top of the three published albums, Joe found enough unreleased material for a fourth. With the Drake family's permission he put together some previously unreleased studio recordings, including Time Of No Reply, Joey, Clothes Of Sand and Mayfair, with some outtakes, some alternative versions, and a few tracks rescued and enhanced from Nick's 'work tape'. In 1987, this album was released in its own right as *Time of No Reply*. Nick Drake now had six albums in the shops.

Rodney and Molly Drake were delighted that their son had finally started to get some recognition. But they both died without seeing the extraordinary explosion of interest in Nick's life and music. Their faithful Karen servant Naw died at the beginning of 1988 and was buried in Tanworth Church on January 31st. Two hymn books were dedicated to Naw and her older relative Rosie, who had also served the Drakes, but they have both disappeared from the church. Rodney Drake, who had a history of heart problems, died soon afterwards aged 79, following a long illness, and his ashes were interred next to his son's in Tanworth on 16 April. Within a few weeks, Molly had abandoned the big house at Far Leys and moved into a pretty cottage called Orchard House on The Green in

Tanworth. She continued to play a big part in village life, especially singing in the choir, and could still be persuaded to perform one of her songs at the piano until well into her 70s. She died on June 7, 1993, at the age of 77, and her name was added to Rodney's and Nick's on the headstone that sits under the big spreading oak tree to the southeast of the Church of St Mary Magdalene. On the rear of the modest stone memorial is a quotation from Nick's song From The Morning: 'now we rise and we are everywhere'.

12. Time Has Told Me

SINCE MOLLY Drake's death the exploitation of the Nick Drake catalogue has continued apace. First, in 1994, came a new compilation to replace *Heaven In A Wild Flower*, which Joe Boyd had never really liked and which had been cut from copy tapes instead of the original studio masters. *Way To Blue*, subtitled *An Introduction To Nick Drake*, contained ten of its predecessor's tracks but also drew from material that had emerged since. Writing in the *NME*, Iestyn George advised a new generation of music consumers to 'go buy this album. It could be the best musical discovery you make this year'. What a change from the reviews Nick was getting during his lifetime.

The name checks were increasing. In 1993, *The Times* chose *Five Leaves Left* as one of its 100 Best Albums of All Time.[106] Stephen Tin Tin Duffy called his band The Lilac Time after a phrase in Nick's song River Man. Matt Johnson of The The compared Nick to Syd Barrett and Tim Buckley in the press release for *Way To Blue*. Ben Watt from Everything But The Girl chose *Five Leaves Left* as one of his favourite albums in *Q* magazine. Kate Bush, Paul Weller, The Cardigans and The Black Crowes all dropped Nick's name in interviews. In

1992, Alan Duffy, who ran the remarkable Imaginary Records label from his bedroom in Manchester, produced *Brittle Days*, the first tribute album to Nick Drake. Named after one of the brief sketches on Nick's work tape, it featured a hotchpotch of lesser-known acts and young bands, from The High Llamas to Clive Gregson, covering Nick's songs. It was an album of variable quality to say the least, but it kept Nick's name in the music papers and on leftfield radio programmes where it could find a new audience.

Also featured on *Brittle Days* was the man who had done more than anyone to keep Nick's name alive in the United States. Scott Appel's versions of From The Morning and Hazey Jane I show how well he had mastered Nick's guitar style, and while his voice may not be to everyone's taste, Nick Drake fans usually acknowledge Appel as one of the best interpreters of their hero's work. Six years younger than Nick, Scott was born in Brooklyn, New York, and died aged just 48 in New Jersey in 2003. While studying at the prestigious Berklee School of Music in Boston he became acquainted with Nick's work, fell in love with it and dedicated most of his life afterwards to popularising it. In 1986 he travelled to England and made friends with Rodney and Molly Drake. They were attracted to this gifted American musician who was familiar with their son's work, and they gave him copies of Nick's work tape and some fragments of lyrics. Appel went home and recorded his own very faithful reconstructions of Bird Flew By, Our Season and Blossom, which Nick had never recorded. Spookily, he also stitched together some other snatches from the work tape with his own themes to create Far Leys, a duet with his long-dead hero. The resultant album, *Nine of Swords*, first released in 1989, was given three and a half stars by *Rolling Stone* and described as 'one of the best albums to be released this year' in *Billboard*. The *LA Times* said it was 'a moving example of an artist realizing his own vision by honouring the achievement of a master'.

Nick's music also began to be featured in tribute concerts. Beginning in the mid-1990s there were dozens on both sides of the Atlantic. One of the biggest was organised by Peter Holsapple, formerly with The dB's and unofficial fifth member of REM, at St Ann's Church in Brooklyn, New York, on November 8, 1997. Musicians included Syd Straw (I Was Made To Love Magic and Pink Moon), Peter Blegvad (Clothes Of Sand) and Terre Roche (Joey and Poor Boy) and the concert was broadcast on WFUV-FM. An even grander event was held at the Barbican Theatre in London on September 25, 1999, as part of a season called English Originals. Kate St John, who had played cor anglais and sung on The Dream Academy's Life In A Northern Town, was musical director of an extraordinary evening, which included interpretations of Nick's songs by Robyn Hitchcock, Beth Orton, Bernard Butler, Jackie Dankworth and the then unknown David Gray. Hitchcock's savage metallic version of Pink Moon had to be heard to be believed, but the stars of the evening were two of Nick's female friends – Robin Frederick, his musical partner from Aix who wrote Been Smokin' Too Long, and Beverley Martyn, who performed her own takes on Magic and Time Has Told Me.

Concerts were fine, but the holy grail for all supporters of Nick's heritage was a television show. The growing number of Drake fans working in the media recognised that his tragic story had all the ingredients for a documentary film. The problem was the lack of footage. There was no film of Nick playing live or talking. There wasn't even a music video. Some ingenious ideas were mooted. In 1996, when I was Head of BBC Music Entertainment, I was approached by a German filmmaker who wanted the BBC to invest in a drama-documentary about Nick, which would be shot bilingually. One UK production company pitched a cartoon treatment of Nick's life. Another came up with a plan to use an animatronic Nick intercut with live action. There was also an attempt by a group that had coalesced around Nick's former sound engineer, John Wood, and his partner in Sound Techniques,[107] Geoff Frost. Back in the 1980s, a young television journalist, Dave Barber, had been captivated by Nick's music when he saw a short item about him from a regional news programme while on a BBC training course. After buying *Heaven In A Wild Flower* and then reading the *Fruit Tree* booklet, he became convinced that there was a fascinating story to tell, so he set about contacting Nick's family and friends. Gabrielle Drake introduced him to her mother and Barber recorded an interview with Molly in her house in Tanworth. He also persuaded John Martyn to share his views on Nick, something no one has managed since. I first knew about Dave Barber's work through the guitarist and singer Clive Gregson, who called me asking if the BBC would like to co-produce the project. I did, but I couldn't interest anyone at BBC1 or BBC2 in showing it. At the same time an article appeared in regional newspapers around Cambridge asking for anyone who knew Nick to contact Dave Barber at Sound Techniques in Mildenhall, Suffolk. Barber was quoted as saying 'We've come about half way through.'

In the end, though, the Sound Techniques consortium was trumped by Tim Clements, a young director working for the BBC in Bristol. He pitched an idea to a BBC2 documentary strand called *Picture This* of a film that would tell Nick's story by reuniting his friends and colleagues, and shooting them in discussion. One group was assembled in Cambridge. 'It was dreadful,' recalls Brian Wells. 'Robert Kirby and I arranged to meet in the Copper Kettle in Cambridge and we sat at the same table for five minutes before we recognised each other. When the camera rolled we had nothing to add.' The session in London with some of Nick's old friends from Aix and Chelsea, including Alex Henderson, Julian and Victoria Lloyd, Ben Laycock and Victoria Waymouth, was more revealing, and a scene where Joe Boyd, Linda Thompson and John Wood listened to a fragment of Molly Drake singing was very striking. Marlborough and Aix friends Simon Crocker and Jeremy Mason were filmed in Jeremy's antiques shop and were dismayed to find that what they thought was an outtake was used in the finished programme. Nevertheless the 40-minute film, *A Stranger Among Us, Searching For Nick Drake*, did take Nick's story and his music on to mainstream television for the first time. Footage was also shot at the 1998 Glastonbury Festival and at the 50th birthday concert in London, and the combination of memories from people who knew Nick with views of young fans who weren't born when he was making music usefully put the Drake legacy in perspective.

Meanwhile, the very persistent Dave Barber had turned his thoughts to radio. He pitched an idea for a documentary about Nick to BBC Radio 2, which was then starting its modernisation under the former Head of BBC TV Light Entertainment, Jim Moir. Coincidentally Moir had produced a comedy show in the 1970s, with the American stand-up Kelly Monteith, which featured Gabrielle Drake as Monteith's wife. The two had kept in touch and in 1997 Gabrielle, by now working tirelessly to increase her brother's profile, took Jim Moir to lunch to try to persuade him to feature more of Nick's music. So when Dave Barber's proposal arrived on his desk, he made the connection. The result was the excellent *Fruit Tree – The Nick Drake Story*, written and produced by Barber, narrated by Nick's friend and occasional bass payer Danny Thompson, and broadcast on Saturday June 20, 1998, at 7pm. The usual suspects – Kirby, Boyd, Wood, Gabrielle – were all there, but for the first time Nick Drake fans heard his parents talking about their son and his tragic story. It was a remarkable programme and it made a big impact on Nick's growing family of admirers.

Newspapers and magazines were now carrying Nick Drake articles as a matter of course. He was still a cult act but, in the UK at least, he could no longer be regarded as unknown. There was even a fanzine, *Pink Moon* (later *Pynk*

Moon), put together by a young Drake fanatic from Walton-on-Thames, Jason Creed. Like many of his generation, Creed found Nick through Paul Weller. Just after Weller's *Wildwood* album had been released he gave an interview to the *NME* where he extolled the virtues of *Five Leaves Left*, which he had been bought as a birthday present. Jason Creed bought *Way To Blue*, then Nick's other albums and in a few months developed, in his words, 'from a fan to an obsessive'. While working at various humdrum jobs in the motor trade and then at college re-taking his GCSE's Creed began by distributing cassettes of Nick's unreleased material and then published his fanzine about four times a year, selling about 500 copies of each issue by mail order. Between 1994 and 1999 there were 19 issues of *Pynk Moon*, containing interviews, appreciations, discographies, old newspaper clippings and photographs. Together they form a remarkable document and it's a pity that after five years Jason Creed decided he'd 'grown out of it' and ceased publication. Fortunately, copies of the magazine can still be found on various Nick Drake websites.

With all the interest in Nick's life and legend, it was inevitable that someone would write a fully fledged biography. Dave Barber had tried, but given up to concentrate on his radio documentary. The Danish poet Gorm Henrik Rasmussen spoke to the Drake family and wrote a 114-page appreciation called 'Pink Moon – Sangeren og guitaristen Nick Drake'[108] in 1980. It was an impressive work, which put Nick's lyrics, including some unpublished songs that Rodney and Molly had showed him, in their literary context. But it sold just 150 copies. There was Lubow's essay from *Fruit Tree* and some notes by Frank Kornellson on *Time Of No Reply*, but it was left to the distinguished music journalist Patrick Humphries to research and write the first exhaustive survey of Nick's background, life and reputation.

As the new millennium dawned, Nick's status had already reached heights he could barely have dreamed of in his own lifetime. Suddenly, though, his career was to really take off. The US advertising agency Arnold had recruited well-known pop video directors Jonathan Dayton and Valerie Faris to shoot a new commercial spot for one of its biggest clients, Volkswagen. The German car maker was releasing a new soft-top version of its popular Golf model and was looking for a film that would enhance the image of the car as a cool, young fashion accessory. For the soundtrack Arnold's creatives had chosen Under The Milky Way by the trippy Australian band The Church, but at the last minute they couldn't clear the song for commercial use. Scrabbling around for an alternative, one of the screenwriters suggested Pink Moon by Nick Drake. 'We were very excited because we were long-term Nick Drake fans,' recalls Jon Dayton. 'It was a really cool idea, it had cachet.' Dayton and Faris, a married couple, approached the task of filming with caution. Dayton says 'sometimes it's treacherous to use music in a commercial. When Nike used Revolution by The Beatles I felt violated. But we used Pink Moon as it could occur in life. We used it to create a feeling. It could have been an ad for a perfume or for any car or even for a car radio. The track wasn't endorsing the product.'

The script for the 30-second spot was simple. Four friends drive through the countryside to a beer joint. Pink Moon is on the car radio. When they get to the roadside bar, they hear shouting and see a drunk in the car park. They look at each other, the car's reversing light comes on and they head off again on the open road as a pink moon illuminates the sky. 'We've directed a lot of music videos, so we shot the song. It was a great chance to "feel the song",' says Dayton. 'The kids knew which song they were listening to.' Cinematography was by Lance Acord, who went on to film the Oscar-nominated *Lost In Translation*, and the ad was shot in Bodega Bay, north of San Francisco. It has a moody and reflective quality with lots of blue shades added in the processing. The moon, sadly, had to be superimposed later. As the spot faded out – there was no voiceover – a caption read 'VW Cabrio Drivers Wanted'. People who watched the spot on the website were invited to click on one of two buttons: Learn About the Car or Purchase the Music. Nick Drake sold more albums in the USA in one month than he had in the previous 30 years and Pink Moon found itself in the Billboard Top 100. The commercial won a number of awards for Dayton and Faris and cemented their reputation as filmmakers. 'I'm very proud of it,' says Jon Dayton. 'Many people in advertising say it's their favourite commercial.' And he still loves Nick's music. 'There's an honesty, a timelessness, a vulnerability and directness that never goes out of style. Fads come and go but he never sounds dated.'

Another filmmaker with a passion for Nick Drake's music and image came out of the Academy of Arts in Breda, Holland, in 1993. It took Jeroen Berkvens seven years to raise the finance and then shoot the haunting impressionistic documentary *A Skin Too Few*, which was premiered in 2000 and has travelled around the world ever since. With money from the Humanist Broadcasting Foundation, Berkvens shot interviews with the prime movers in Nick's story and added dreamy shots of the countryside around Tanworth while Nick's songs played on the soundtrack. Tim Clements' film had done the same, but several things made Berkvens' film very different. First he persuaded John Wood and Robert Kirby to revisit the master tape of At The Chime Of A City Clock from *Bryter Layter* and strip it down so viewers could hear the way individual tracks had been mixed to create the whole. Then, with advice from Gabrielle Drake, Berkvens recreated Nick's bedroom at Far Leys as it had been when he died. It could have been teeth-grindingly schmaltzy, but he carried it off superbly. Dennis Harvey's review in the *LA Times* says it all: 'Given the alarming lack of material to draw on, Berkvens does a very difficult, admirable thing: his documentary often eschews facts and commentary to try evoking mysterious Nickdom. This stuff should be boring, but it's so beautifully measured and crafted that it carries a hypnotic, lyrical gravity instead.'

Towards the end of the filming with Gabrielle Drake, Jeroen Berkvens hit paydirt. Idly looking around the room while Nick's sister was talking he saw some old film spools on a shelf. On closer inspection one had a label that said 'Family Holiday'. 'Would Nick be on that?', asked Jeroen. 'Oh yes, probably,' said his sister. And thus emerged the first, and as yet, only moving pictures of Nick Drake. In the first sequence he's a baby in his mother's arms being admired by his father and the Karen nanny Rosie. Later we see him playing happily at the seaside with Gabrielle and his parents, a far cry from the mournful figure on the beach near Harlech that adorns the sleeve of the Hannibal *Fruit Tree*.

A Skin Too Few was aired by the digital channel BBC4 on Saturday May 22, 2004. In the same month BBC Radio 2 broadcast an updated version of Dave Barber's 1998 documentary, now retitled *Lost Boy: In Search Of Nick Drake* with a new voiceover by no less a narrator than Brad Pitt. Barber, now working full-time for the network, had read reports that the film star and Jennifer Aniston had asked for some of Nick's music to be played at their sumptuous Malibu wedding celebration in July 2000. He contacted Brad Pitt's LA management and within days was on his way to Hollywood to record the new narration for the programme. It was a huge coup for Barber, and the attendant publicity, for both Radio 2 and Nick Drake, was enormous. Nick's name finally made the front pages of the tabloid newspapers. Featured in the revised documentary was the song Tow The Line, which John Wood had recently discovered while remixing all of Nick's albums in the new 5.1 surround format. Joe Boyd isn't convinced that the undiscovered song actually dates from Nick's final session, and Ross Grainger remembers Nick singing it live in 1969, but John Wood is adamant. For the 2004 album release *Made To Love Magic*, he left the track running after the final note so we can all hear Nick putting down his guitar for the final time. It makes for a moving sign-off. The sleeve design for the CD includes a handwritten sheet of the lyrics showing that Nick certainly spelt 'tow' with a 'w', although it's most probably a simple spelling mistake. To 'toe the line' meaning to conform to the rules, is exactly the kind of quaint English expression that Nick used, like 'when day is done'.

Made To Love Magic included enough unreleased tracks to excite Nick's fans, but also enough familiar material to risk accusations of exploitation. The four tracks from 1974 were included again, as were Joey, Clothes Of Sand and the outtake of The Thoughts Of Mary Jane, which had appeared on the *Time Of No Reply* album. But the previously unheard versions of River Man and Mayfair, recorded in 1968 by Robert Kirby on his Ferrograph at Caius College, were a treat. Also fascinating for Nick Drake completists were Magic and Time Of No Reply itself, where Robert Kirby had dug out his old string arrangements and re-recorded them with Nick's original vocal tracks. Magic[109] was even released as a single, Nick's first, and with the help of Brad Pitt's profile and the first properly organised marketing campaign for one of his records, Nick scored his first bona fide hit, spending one week in the UK Top 40 at number 35. The compilation sold well, too, and quickly became Nick's best-selling album. Thirty years after his death he was finally getting the attention he deserved.

This flurry of activity with Nick's music coincided with the end of Joe Boyd's distribution deal through his Hannibal label and the takeover of Island Records by the giant Universal group. To spearhead a more businesslike campaign Gabrielle Drake had appointed sleeve designer and former manager of Julian Cope, Cally von Callomon, as director of Bryter Music, The Nick Drake Estate, with a mission to continue popularising the brand. A long-standing Nick Drake fan who had spent time as creative director of Island Records in the 1990s, Cally set about his task with missionary zeal.

Hot on the heels of the *Made To Love Magic* album came *A Treasury*, another 'best of' compilation to replace *Way To Blue*. All the tracks had been available previously, but to tempt fans to buy them all again, Cally added an uncredited recording of Nick playing Plaisir D'Amour 34 seconds after the end of the official final track From The Morning. It's a lovely piece of guitar playing and a memorable example of Nick's clean, ringing style, but the words 'rip-off' started to appear on Nick Drake message boards. It was asking a lot of Nick's loyal fans to buy an entire CD to own one 46-second instrumental. Many supporters were also horrified by the decision to make a promo video for River Man, which was to become Nick's second single. Cally recruited Tim Pope, one of the great music directors of the 1980s, who shot some dreamy slow-motion sequences on Hampstead Heath and cut them together with some of Keith Morris's original black-and-white portraits. Towards the end of the video, Nick's eyes are made to move within one of shots from the final photo session at Hampstead Ponds. It's a spooky and nerve-tingling moment as Nick seems fleetingly to come back to life.

Afterword

SO DID IT all have to be this way? Could anything have been done to rescue Nick from his despair and decline? Well yes, probably. Rodney and Molly Drake were a prosperous couple who spoiled their only son and gave him everything he wanted except the freedom to be himself. Like most parents of young people in the turbulent 1960s they had no idea what was going on in their boy's head. They had no relevant life experience to help them deal with a child who broke all their rules and defied all their conventions. After his death their respect for him began to grow as they discovered how popular his music was becoming, but during his adult lifetime, they were anything but encouraging of his musical ambitions. They allowed him to feel guilty about not wanting to grow up in their world with their ideals and ambitions. His sister Gabrielle has acknowledged that she too lost patience with Nick during his darkest times when he must have been very trying company. And his friends must accept some responsibility for the abject condition into which Nick was allowed to sink. Someone might have noticed that he was smoking too much cannabis and experimenting with other drugs that didn't seem to be doing him any good. But as in the cases of Peter Green and Syd Barrett, it just wasn't cool to get involved with people's personal trips, man. It didn't help that Nick could be stand-offish and wary of close friendship, but some of his friends have admitted that they could have done more to support him emotionally during his final years.

Joe Boyd has acknowledged in recent interviews that his management style had a part to play in Nick's decline. That first contract, giving Joe complete control over his career, was not the deal an artist like Nick needed. He should have had independent advice from a manager about his record deal, and independent advice from a record company about a producer. It would have helped if different people had been able to look after his publishing and his live work. Perhaps then he wouldn't have been allowed to make an album, *Bryter Layter*, that overwhelmed him. And perhaps he wouldn't have been pushed to the limit of his endurance on the road, touring without even a guitar roadie or a driver. When Joe Boyd turned tail and headed back to Hollywood in 1972, Nick had no one to turn to and nowhere to go. He was still under contract to a man who wasn't there. So when the disillusionment turned to despair, he was quite alone.

Was Nick mentally ill? The evidence is sparse and inconclusive, but I think he was. Nick's behaviour over a long period is highly suggestive of a cannabis-fuelled psychosis, a mild schizophrenia, which a combination of prescribed and illicit drugs did nothing to cure and most probably worsened. The depression into which Nick fell was not one he could climb out of himself. There are indications that he tried and that he was frustrated by his condition, but he could never manage to shake off the black-eyed dog. And in his case, the drugs didn't work. 'If I had a patient like Nick today,' Dr Brian Wells told me, 'I would treat them with cognitive behavioural therapy rather than antidepressant drugs. I would send them to an experiential treatment centre where you climb ropes and mix with people and get some confidence.' It might have worked.

Two other issues recurred many times during the interviews for this book and are regularly chewed over on the websites and chat rooms about Nick that have proliferated in the last few years. The first is simply dealt with. Was Nick gay? Tony Reif, the Canadian musician who organised the Poor Boy concert in Canada and the subsequent album of jazz versions of Nick's songs, wrote a long paper advocating the theory and remains convinced that he was at least bisexual. Other people have speculated that Nick was sexually attracted to photographer Keith Morris, to Joe Boyd and to John Martyn. There is also a story that Nick had a boyfriend in Paris and that his final happier days in the summer of 1974 were spent coming out. But it is much more likely that something in Nick's psyche prevented him from fully expressing physical emotions of any sort. The cool air of studied mystery that people noted at Eagle House, at Marlborough, in Aix and in London disguised a reservation about physicality that must have been particularly uncomfortable to bear in the era of free love. His disdain for the girl in Aix who had sex with multiple partners, his remarks to Peter Rice at Cambridge about Jim Morrison being 'too raw, too explicit', his inability or unwillingness to consummate his romance with Linda Thompson, all point to a man who was uneasy about sex. Brian Wells, who knew him as well as anyone, told me, 'I can't really imagine Nick having sex with anyone because he would have to take his clothes off and he was always far too shy to do that.'

The other question is whether there was anything in Nick's childhood that might have manifested itself later on in the withdrawn and distracted behaviour he exhibited in his final years? Did something come before the cannabis, the acid trips and the heroin to start his downward spiral? The word 'compartmentalisation' keeps cropping up in interviews with Nick's friends and colleagues. He liked to keep people he knew in discrete boxes where they couldn't touch each other, and perhaps where they couldn't compare notes about him. That word is also common in discussions of the effects of childhood trauma on adults in later life. Lack of self-esteem, difficulty maintaining relationships, drug addiction, a sense of childhood magic being taken away, a death wish, they are all symptoms reported by victims of abuse. In Nick's case the published evidence points overwhelmingly to what his sister Gabrielle has called an 'idyllic childhood' and it would be irresponsible to raise unsubstantiated rumours about Nick's upbringing.[110] But the speculation will continue because the evidence of Nick's own lyrics is compelling. Time Has Told Me, River Man (especially with the 'missing' verse), Magic,

Hazey Jane I, Fly, Fruit Tree, Place To Be, Cello Song, all of them fit the child abuse template.

So did Nick want to die? Was he so unhappy, so ill at ease within himself that the suicide was part of a plan that, as Joe Boyd has suggested, he hatched in his youth? The evidence of his earliest lyrics, especially Fruit Tree, is compelling. This was an era when suicide and early death were on the agenda. Jimi Hendrix, Janis Joplin, Jim Morrison and others brought a morbidity to the conversations of musicians at the time, and there seemed to be something gloriously romantic about uniting a narcotic-fuelled search for nirvana with the end of physical being. I think of Nick Drake as a latter-day Thomas Chatterton, England's first romantic poet, who took his own life in 1770, aged just 17.[111] Like Chatterton, Nick couldn't cope with failure. He knew that his personality and his talent had not equipped him for either the world his father intended for him or the career he had chosen for himself. As he got older, sadder and less physically fit, the attraction of ending the struggle became overwhelming. If it hadn't happened on November 25, 1974, it would probably have happened soon afterwards.

What would have become of him if he'd lived? It's tempting to imagine David Geffen riding to Nick's rescue and adding him to the Asylum Records roster alongside Jackson Browne and, briefly, Bob Dylan. Geffen certainly took an interest in Nick's career and has claimed that he tried to sign him in 1972, but was thwarted by Joe Boyd and Island. Perhaps Nick might have ended up in a Bel Air or Malibu mansion writing film music like one of his heroes, Randy Newman. Elton John told me that Nick would definitely have prospered in 1970s America and might have made symphonic albums like David Ackles' *American Gothic*, which was produced by Elton's writing partner Bernie Taupin. Maybe the more reverential folk clubs and student bars of the United States would have helped Nick conquer his dislike of live performance and his disdain for disrespectful audiences. He would also have had the security of the Wolseley millions, the 'safety net' he had rejected all those years before. None of those places, however, seem to fulfil his stated requirements for 'A Place To Be'.

Things might have been different if he'd been born a couple of decades later. In the 1980s, Nick would never have had to worry about playing live. It's easy to imagine him hard at work in his bedroom or in the music room of Far Leys surrounded by computers, synthesisers and all manner of recording and composing aids that would have been unimaginable in the 1960s. He would probably have made his music on his own and emailed it to a record company or even distributed it himself via the Internet. That sense of mystery would have appealed to him and also suited his diffidence about publicity.

And the future? It surely won't be long before Nick's work starts appearing in exam syllabuses alongside his own heroes like Blake, Tennyson and Wilfred Owen. Nick's Cambridge supervision partner, John Venning, has already studied the Drake oeuvre with some of his students and finds that they react positively. Commercially, expect more Nick Drake releases, including the promised *Family Tree* collection featuring songs by his mother, Molly, more tribute concerts, possibly a movie about Nick's life and probably an officially endorsed biography. With his sister in charge, the Nick Drake industry is in full swing. 'Wretched boy!', she told the *Daily Telegraph* in 2004. 'Here I am, still doing his publicity.' She was joking, of course, but it's clear when you meet her that Nick's sister takes the job of managing the estate very seriously and devotes a lot of her time and energy to it. She doesn't always win admirers among Nick's old friends for her apparently relentless pursuit of a higher profile for Nick's music, more record sales and more revenue for the Estate. One thing is for certain though, Gabrielle Drake is proud of her role as her brother's keeper.

The rest of us have Nick's music, a tiny bittersweet body of work that can calm us, comfort us, sometimes annoy us, but constantly delight and intrigue us. He wasn't always a likeable man and his self-absorption makes some of his lyrics hard to take, but the combination of that voice, that guitar technique and that atmosphere is unique in music. All artists construct the world as they see it and we are fortunate indeed to be allowed into Nick's. William Blake said, 'I must create a system or be controlled by another man's.' Nick Drake understood this and, like Blake, created his own vision, his own symbols and his own myths. From the metaphysical poets like George Herbert and John Donne, he took the idea of codifying the temporal world, using metaphor and allegory, and using words with double and triple meanings. From jazz he took freeform modal structures that ask more questions than they answer, and from the acoustic folk tradition he took a powerful rhythmic engine to propel his music. As Robyn Hitchcock says, 'Nick Drake made a dreamy, fatalistic model that took 20-odd years to fly, but is now working better than ever.'

Acknowledgements

Special thanks go to Dr. Brian Wells who gave up a lot of his (very expensive) time to help me understand Nick's personality as well as the drugs and depression which overwhelmed him, to Iain Cameron whose musicological guidance was inspirational, to Robert Kirby who filled in many missing details from Nick's musical career, and to Sophia Ryde who spoke about Nick on the record for the first time.

Many of my predecessors on the journalistic trail of Nick Drake were generous with their time and their contacts books. Thanks to the pioneering Patrick Humphries and Sue Parr, to Gorm Henrik Rasmussen, to Pete Paphides of the Observer, to Mick Brown of the Telegraph, to Pete Frame, to Jason Creed of Pynk Moon, to Larry Ayres and to BBC Radio 2's Dave Barber.

In Tanworth-in-Arden the Reverend Tim Harmer was unstinting in his assistance. Ray Crabtree gave me an insight into the Drake's family life and John Saunders and Andrew Hicks offered some priceless detail about life at Hurst House.

Thanks also to Margaret and Glenn Holt, June Flavell, Ashley Bent and Margaret Twigg.

Nick 'the captain' Stewart, gave me invaluable detail about Eagle House. Dennis Silk, Randall Keynes and Andy Murison helped me with Marlborough College and the redoubtable Simon Crocker and Jeremy Mason painted a vivid portrait of Nick's life at Marlborough and in Aix. Richard Charkin took me through the events of Nick's Moroccan adventure.

For background on Nick's time at Cambridge I'm indebted to his tutor Dr. Ray Kelly, to Carol Lamb, Emma Camps and Christopher Pratt at Fitzwilliam College, to his supervisor Chris Bristow, his Director of Studies Professor Dominic Baker-Smith, the Cambridgeshire historian Mike Petty and to Nick's contemporaries Peter Rice, Paul Wheeler, John Venning, Professor David Punter, Ed Gilchrist, Colin Fleetcroft, Joe Cobbe and Mike Schutzer-Weissman.

Ashley Hutchings recounted his discovery of Nick and helped to place it on the right date. Joe Boyd was obliging about his role in Nick's career. Keith Morris, who sadly died while this book was in production, was charming and very informative about the photo sessions. Geoff Frost and Dave Pegg gave me a lot of detail about the Sound Techniques studio. Others who helped me with Nick's time in London were Jerry Gilbert, Chris Blackwell, Muff Winwood, Rob Partridge, Alex Henderson, Julian Lloyd, Roy Harper, Dr.Ross Grainger, Bruce Fursman, Herman Gilligan, Mike Appleton, Tony Cox and Sir Elton John. Linda Thompson was remarkably candid about her relationship with Nick.

Jonathan Dayton gave me a fascinating account of how Nick's music reached the MTV generation. Contemporary Drake lovers who helped me understand his enduring appeal included Robert Smith of The Cure, Jeroen Berkvens, Tony Reif, Clive Gregson, Denise Offringa, Mark Pavey, Gilbert Isbin, Stuart Villaroel of the High Planets, Shaun 'Shivering Goat' Hutchinson and Keith James. A big thank you too to Robyn Hitchcock for his quotable quotes.

Thanks too for help and support from John Williams, Mark Cooper and Simon Mayo at the BBC, Mark Ellen and David Hepworth of Word magazine, Joe Levy of Rolling Stone, Simon Garfield, Nick Barraclough, John Leonard, the staff at Cambridge University Library and of course the mighty Ashwell Accies.

This is my first book and I'll always be grateful to Albert DePetrillo, who asked me to write it, to my literary agent Kate Haldane for her encouragement, to my wife Maureen, who persuaded me I could really do it, and my children Celia and Henry, who tolerated my long absences in the office.

I was surprised and delighted by the number of people who were prepared to give up their time to talk about Nick's life and music. Anything good in this book is down to them. The mistakes are mine. If you would like to put anything right or contribute any information for the second edition please email me at ilps9105@aol.com.

Trevor Dann
Cambridge, 2005

Discography

FIVE LEAVES LEFT (1969)

TIME HAS TOLD ME

Nick Drake	vocal, acoustic guitar
Paul Harris	piano
Richard Thompson	electric guitar
Danny Thompson	bass

One of the most assured openings to any debut album, this deceptively simple waltz was many people's introduction to Nick's music when it appeared on the Island sampler *Nice Enough To Eat* in 1969. Richard Thompson's precise, almost Jerry Garcia-style, electric guitar and Danny Thompson's sensuous double bass give the track a west-coast flavour, but the dominant sounds are Nick's robust rhythm guitar, played in a CGCFCE tuning, and his breathy, well-enunciated and very English vocals. The only instrument out of place is the rather lumpy piano. The lyrics work as a simple love song, but other interpretations have suggested an oblique 'coming out' or a subconscious reference to a deep childhood trauma.

RIVER MAN

Nick Drake	vocal, acoustic guitar
Harry Robinson	string arrangement

This remarkable piece is at the core of Nick Drake's timeless appeal. Musicians notice that it's played in 5/4 time (the same as Dave Brubeck's modern jazz standard Take Five) with that eccentric CGCFCE tuning, but most listeners are simply carried along on the wave of melancholia created by Harry Robinson's misty, swirling arrangement, of which Delius would have been proud. The lyric is dark and mysterious, full of bleak allusions. Quite who the mysterious Betty might be we're not told, but there's more than a passing resemblance to the character of Betty Foy, the mother in Wordsworth's poem 'The Idiot Boy', which Nick studied at Cambridge. In a missing verse printed on the album sleeve Nick says that Betty 'hadn't time to smile or die in style but still she tries'. Elsewhere the lost lyric mentions 'where teacher taught and father flies', encouraging more speculation about something in Nick's childhood that he was trying to hide. There's an unmistakeable sense of loss and foreboding, as though the River Man might be death itself. An early version recorded by Robert Kirby at Caius College in 1968 appeared on *Made To Love Magic* in 2004.

THREE HOURS

Nick Drake	vocal, acoustic guitar
Danny Thompson	bass
Rocki Dzidzornu	congas

Mistakenly titled Sundown on the inside of the original gatefold sleeve, this is the song Nick's friend Jeremy Mason claims is dedicated to him. He says Nick confirmed this when they met, but refused to say why and what the lyric is about. Mason supposes that it's something to do with his insatiable appetite for women ('in search of a master, in search of slave') and points out that Jacomo (Giacomo) was Casanova's first name. But it seems more likely that Nick was referring to the master/slave, dominant/submissive dialectic in Hegel's philosophy. Curiously, like River Man, the published lyrics on the initial vinyl release also contain a missing verse, where Nick speaks of 'one hope of failure' turning for the best and three hours taking 'the hope of success'. This was the second attempt to record the song. The first, with a flute part, emerged on the *Made To Love Magic* album. This more considered version features Nick's strong rhythm guitar pattern (DADGAD) enhanced by Danny Thompson's driving bass and congas played by the African percussionist Rocki (Kwase) Dzidzornu.

WAY TO BLUE

Nick Drake	vocal, acoustic guitar
Robert Kirby	string arrangement

Originally intended as the title track for the album, Way To Blue features a sumptuous Robert Kirby arrangement over which Nick's voice sweeps and soars in a style reminiscent of Colin Blunstone on The Zombies' Rose For Emily. The lyric has another searching and questioning theme, very redolent of its era. This is the track that convinced Joe Boyd and John Wood that Kirby was a genius.

DAY IS DONE

Nick Drake	vocal, acoustic guitar
Robert Kirby	string arrangement

Bootleg versions of the first recording with Richard Hewson's orchestration reveal the song slowed to a funereal pace and the guitar buried by lugubrious strings. But the second session, with Robert Kirby's bright Eleanor Rigby-influenced string-quartet arrangement, skips along behind Nick's clever acoustic guitar picking. Lyrically, it's another song about regret and missed chances with Shakespearian hints of the aftermath of a great battle and 'no time to start anew'. The *Fruit Tree* box mistakenly transcribes the line 'newspaper blown across the court' as 'you sped the ball across the court'. Elton John's rocked-up piano version on the Warlock sampler is a joy.

CELLO SONG

Nick Drake	vocal, acoustic guitar
Clare Lowther	cello
Danny Thompson	bass
Rocki Dzidzornu	congas

A stunning guitar intro played on EADF#BE launches the most perfect track on Nick's debut album, a gorgeous blend of double bass and congas with the session player Clare Lowther's cello sharing parts of Nick's hummed melody line. The puzzling lyrics address a character who had 'dreams when so young' and is now 'in the cloud'. Nick sings about the 'armies of emotion' going out to fight while the subject sails to the sky. It may be another lament for the loss of his own childhood innocence.

THE THOUGHTS OF MARY JANE

Nick Drake	vocal, acoustic guitar
Robert Kirby	string arrangement

A slight song, using the same tuning as Cello Song, this was recorded three times before Nick was satisfied. The first version, released on two later compilation albums, included some rather hesitant electric guitar improvisations by Richard Thompson. Then Richard Hewson slowed the tempo and added a syrupy orchestration. Finally, Robert Kirby scored it for flute and a string quartet, and Nick's thinly disguised reference to marijuana found itself a comfortable setting. Like Betty in River Man, Mary Jane is another spiritual, intangible woman, 'the princess of the sky' who tells 'her story to the wind'.

MAN IN A SHED

Nick Drake	vocal, acoustic guitar
Paul Harris	piano
Danny Thompson	bass

By Nick's standards, this is a fairly conventional love song about a poor man aspiring to the company of a woman who lives in a 'house so very big and grand'. He states directly that 'the man is me and the girl is you', but there's none of the darkness that infuses his later tales of unrequited love. An early guitar-only version was released on *Time Of No Reply*. For this take, jazz and blues specialist Paul Harris was employed to add a jaunty piano part alongside Nick's swing-time DGDGDG rhythm.

FRUIT TREE

Nick Drake	vocal, acoustic guitar
Robert Kirby	string arrangement

Nick's death-wish song, almost his mission statement. Not yet 21 years old he's convinced that he won't be recognised until he's dead. Like the fruit tree of the title, his reputation won't flourish until 'its stock [not 'stalk' as some transcriptions have it] is in the ground'. When he's deep in the earth, that's when we'll know what he was really worth. People will stand and stare when he's gone. Darkness gives the brightest light. It's a bleak and pitiless prediction set to a restless melody played on a BBDGBE tuning and augmented by Robert Kirby's plaintive, bittersweet orchestration.

SATURDAY SUN

Nick Drake	vocal, piano
Danny Thompson	bass
Tristan Fry	drums, vibraphone

Classical percussionist Tristan Fry, later a member of the classical/rock fusion band Sky, overdubbed a silky late-night vibraphone part to the album's jazzy coda, which Nick wrote and performed on the piano. Sunday is the day of rain contrasting with the promise of Saturday's sunshine, which brought out people who 'were really too good in their way'.

BRYTER LAYTER (1970)

INTRODUCTION

Nick Drake	acoustic guitar
Dave Pegg	bass guitar
Dave Mattacks	drums
Robert Kirby	string arrangement

This gentle melody was one of Nick's favourite tunes. He was determined that *Bryter Layter* should include the three instrumentals, and refuted accusations that they were only needed as fillers because he hadn't written enough songs. He worked for hours on unusual tunings and enjoyed this one particularly even though there was a serious risk of breaking a string by tightening the top two by a tone or more to DADGDF#, an open D chord. The strong right hand does the work while the left frets one string at a time to improvise a melody around a D chord. You can imagine Nick la-la'ing a basic tune for Robert Kirby to develop into the sweeping string arrangement that would have fitted easily into *Five Leaves Left*.

HAZEY JANE II

Nick Drake	vocal, acoustic guitar
Dave Pegg	bass guitar
Dave Mattacks	drums
Richard Thompson	lead guitar
Robert Kirby	brass arrangement

A rude musical awakening for any listener lulled by the overture into expecting Nick's second album to be another gentle, pastoral one like his first. Nick strums instead of finger-picking. There's a pumping brass arrangement by Kirby, echoing James Last or even Herb Alpert, and a jaunty folk-rock bass guitar instead of a languid jazzy double bass. And drums – drums on a Nick Drake album for goodness sake! Nick's vocal is a shock too – for the lover of River Man or Way To Blue there are too many words tumbling over each other. The precise and perfectionist Nick even runs out of breath before the end of the first verse, struggling to hit the right note on the word 'morning'. The kitchen-sink-and-all production doesn't even allow Richard Thompson's gentle noodling to penetrate the sessionman swamp. It's making a statement about the compromises of the second album: this one is intended to be different, more approachable, more contemporary, more radio-friendly. Fortunately, after the initial shock, the splendour of the song emerges. Based on the same tuning as Introduction, though capo'd up a tone, it is one of Nick's great melodies and includes one of his best-known and most revealing lyrics – the one about the situation being fine if only songs were lines in a conversation. There has been much speculation about the identity of Jane. Is she a girlfriend – perhaps Sophia Ryde? Is she a catchall for the dissolute and dysfunctional women who were floating in and out of his life at this time. Or is Hazey Jane part of the thought process that gave us Mary Jane on *Five Leaves Left* – has the marijuana been replaced by heroin? (By the way, we must forgive 'weigh up' instead of 'weigh' your anchor as we forgive the later misspelling of 'toe the line'.)

AT THE CHIME OF A CITY CLOCK

Nick Drake	vocal, acoustic guitar
Ray Warleigh	alto sax
Dave Pegg	bass guitar
Mike Kowalski	drums
Robert Kirby	string and brass arrangement

The metropolitan cityscape lyric and unsettling major-to-minor chord structure make it clear that *Five Leaves Left*'s man in a shed is now *Bryter Layter*'s man in a cold bedsit. A jazzy shuffle rhythm, which in another setting might suggest Jobim's Girl From Ipanema, is the backdrop to an essay on urban alienation inspired by Nick's experiences of late 1960s London. He may have been influenced by Donovan's Sunny Goodge Street on his 1965 album *Fairy Tale*, which has a similar feel, a Kirby-style cello and flute arrangement by Terry Kennedy and a comparably dark, melancholic mood. Nick may also have been thinking of some of the themes in William Blake's *Songs Of Innocence And Experience*. It's a jungle out there and even those who think they know how to cope are struggling. The Shakespearian military themes of Day Is Done and Cello Song re-emerge in the lines about hanging on to your crown and the city man who leaves his armour down. Ray Warleigh's chilling alto sax improvisation comes straight from a gangster movie soundtrack and enhances the feelings of loneliness, rejection and desolation. The tuning is conventional but dropped a semi-tone. Check out Iain Cameron's fascinating essay (available at http://www.algonet.se/~iguana/DRAKE/RM&ATC.html), which explores the structure of this song in exhaustive detail. Finicky listeners may enjoy the little mistake by the session drummer Mike Kowalski, a member of The Beach Boys' live band, at 2'50". No one seems to notice, so he carries on regardless.

ONE OF THESE THINGS FIRST

Nick Drake	vocal, acoustic guitar
Paul Harris	piano
Ed Carter	bass guitar
Mike Kowalski	drums

Nick tunes his fourth string up a tone to create an EAEGBE tuning and a deceptively cheerful rolling landscape for a soliloquy about failure and under-achievement. It's the musical version of his statement to his mother Molly that he'd failed in everything he'd ever tried to do. Here, he could, he should, he would have been and done lots of things but – and this is intriguing – there is no but. There is no description of how he feels now or what he might be able to do to rectify the situation, just a lament about missed opportunities and lost happiness with no optimism, no solutions and no hope. In Dave Pegg's absence, Ed Carter, another member of The Beach Boys' band, contributed a bass part, which Peggy was very proud of until he read the sleeve notes many years later: 'Oh shit, it's not me!' Paul Harris's overdubbed and rather too sprightly piano is the dominant instrument on another track that might have benefited from a more spartan production and more rehearsal time.

HAZEY JANE I

Nick Drake	vocal, acoustic guitar
Dave Pegg	bass guitar
Dave Mattacks	drums
Robert Kirby	string arrangement

A finger-picked flourish on the now-familiar DADGDF# tuning launches another reflection on life and its futility. Even more than Hazey Jane II, the lyric sustains the theory about heroin being an inspiration. On the languorous demo version from the work tape Nick is clearly stoned on something. It could be the drug that's riding the man who looks a little like him in the last verse. But like the Far Leys monologue it's possible that he's simply talking to himself. 'Do you curse where you come from', he asks in the opening line. Is he a remnant of things past? Are things moving just a little too fast? These were questions Nick had asked himself all his life and were becoming more pertinent during that cold lonely winter in Belsize Park. Robert Kirby's melancholic strings and the restless drum mallets and cymbal crashes of Fairport's Dave Mattacks complement one of Nick's most assured vocal performances. John Wood cleverly lets all the instrumentation fade out before the final acoustic guitar coda. Beautiful.

BRYTER LAYTER

Nick Drake	acoustic guitar
Lyn Dobson	flute
Dave Pegg	bass guitar
Dave Mattacks	drums
Robert Kirby	string arrangement

In those vinyl days this was the first track on side 2, another instrumental like the opening to side 1, but more than twice as long and not even half as good. The opening flute melody sounds like the signature tune to an ancient BBC radio series or the soundtrack to an education programme about wild flowers. But the laboured string section is worse. Supermarkets have played less bland music than this. Lyn Dobson's Tull-style improvised flute towards the end nearly saves the track, but its removal would not have spoiled the album at all. To make it the title track was positively perverse.

FLY

Nick Drake	vocal, acoustic guitar
John Cale	viola, harpsichord
Dave Pegg	bass guitar

As with the opening two tracks on the album, Fly uses the same tuning as its preceding instrumental. This may explain the sequencing of the original album. But Nick's impassioned plea for a second chance is one of the sublime moments of *Bryter Layter* and surely deserved greater prominence. The slowly descending bass notes of the tune pre-echo a similar structure on Pink Moon. 'Please,' implores Nick before the melody starts its inexorable fall, carrying the implication that his requests won't be answered and his wishes will remain unfulfilled. John Cale's harpsichord is too prominent in the mix for some tastes, but his overdubbed viola part is superb, doing the same job as Clare Lowther's cello in *Five Leaves Left*'s Cello Song. The published words state that 'it's really too hard for to fly' but Nick occasionally seems to sing that it's really too hard for the fly. Either way it's another sumptuous melancholic three minutes and shows that, despite any of Nick's later reservations, John Cale understood where his music was coming from. Several early versions of Fly exist on bootlegs and there's one from the work tape on *Time Of No Reply*, but for once the additional instruments add to rather than subtract from the brilliance of the raw song.

POOR BOY

Nick Drake	vocal, acoustic guitar
Ray Warleigh	alto sax
Chris McGregor	piano
Dave Pegg	bass guitar
Mike Kowalski	drums
Pat Arnold	backing vocal
Doris Troy	backing vocal

Nick loved this. So did Chris McGregor of The Brotherhood Of Breath, who knew a thing or two about avant-garde jazz piano. But to modern ears it's an over-fussy setting for a rather slight song, which finds Nick feeling sorry for himself and actually saying so in so many words. Nick seems to be playing an electric guitar; either that or his acoustic has been treated to sound like one. The tuning is conventional EADGBE. Ray Warleigh's alto sax is terrific but some listeners find the backing vocals by PP Arnold and Doris Troy phoney. The stark unembellished version on the work tape is immensely superior. On that one Nick is at the end of his tether and it shows. This buffed-up commercial version has even given one critic cause to ask whether Nick was poking fun at himself. Not if you listen to the original. The line about being keen to take a wife shouldn't be taken literally.

NORTHERN SKY

Nick Drake	vocal, acoustic guitar
John Cale	celeste, piano, organ
Dave Pegg	bass guitar
Mike Kowalski	drums

The simple love song that inspired Nick Laird-Clowes of The Dream Academy to write Life In A Northern Town, a Top 10 US and UK hit in 1985, could have been Nick Drake's hit single. It was another strange decision by producer Joe Boyd to bury it away near the end of side 2. The melody, set over another of Nick's favourite tunings, DADGDG, is gorgeous, the singing enchanting and achingly honest, and the setting by John Cale, opulent without overpowering the fragile little song. The stop-start middle section sounds more Cale than Drake but it shows how a musical collaborator might have stimulated Nick to develop had he lived. More than 30 years after it was recorded, *New Musical Express* called this the 'greatest English love song of modern times' and many people say that it's Nick's finest achievement. It's certainly been 'our tune' for more than a few couples over the years. Beverley Martyn has said that Northern Sky was written in Hastings at the house she shared with husband John. Nick used to stay in a room where he could see the ocean through the top of a tree. But was it written for Beverley, to whom Nick was very close? Or Linda Peters (Thompson)? Or Sophia Ryde? Or could it be another drug song? Again, the lyrics allow any number of interpretations so we can take our choice or find something of our own in them.

SUNDAY

Nick Drake	acoustic guitar
Ray Warleigh	flute
Dave Pegg	bass guitar
Dave Mattacks	drums
Robert Kirby	string arrangement

The third instrumental on the album has a prestigious place in the sequencing, like the other two. After using non-vocal tracks to open both sides, here was Joe Boyd (or possibly Nick himself) placing a likeable but eminently disposable piece of what film directors call 'library music' at the end of side 2 where rock fans expected to find the album's *meisterwerk*, its A Day In The Life or Are You Experienced. Instead we get more supermarket muzak, good enough for a documentary soundtrack but an unsatisfactorily bland and insipid ending to an album of such rich emotion and deep torment.

PINK MOON (1971)

All songs: Nick Drake
               vocal and acoustic guitar
               piano on title track

PINK MOON

Nick shows the influence of his friend John Martyn as he slurs his way into a simple lyric about impending danger and complacency. He 'zaw it written' that the pink moon is on its way and it's 'gonna get ye all'. The guitar is strummed and the tuning, DADGDF#, is, perhaps intentionally, too low for Nick's range so that as he reaches the end of the descending scale he can't quite hit the note. The haunting piano overdub is quite beautiful and demonstrates a musicality that's missing from some of the bleaker pieces on the third album.

PLACE TO BE

The version on Nick's work tape from 1969 suggests that this song was intended for *Five Leaves Left*. It's another deeply introspective song, self-referential in the line about day being done, and descriptive of the despair into which Nick was falling. Like Man In A Shed it can be read as a simple tale of unrequited love but the mood has darkened and Nick seems once again to be hinting at a dark secret in his past.

ROAD

The very complex finger-picking on a DGDDAD tuning shows that Nick's guitar technique was still at its best during the *Pink Moon* sessions. Equally, the lyrics show that he was less concerned with the poetic images and literary allusions of his earlier songs. He can take a road that'll see him through. Suicide perhaps?

WHICH WILL

In earlier times, Nick would have asked for another take of this song to correct the tiny slip in his finger-picking just before the end. But by the time of *Pink Moon* he was less inclined to bother with perfection. The tuning, BF#BEBD#, is one Nick hadn't used before and wouldn't use again. Lyrically the song follows the by now well-worn path of abandonment and disillusionment.

HORN

Barely 75 seconds long, this instrumental is played on the second and third strings only, with the fourth left to resonate in C major. Nick may be recalling the music he had heard in Morocco. On the horn of the title, the melody would work as a call to prayer. On the mournful, echoing acoustic guitar it becomes a chilling lament.

THINGS BEHIND THE SUN

The longest and most lyrically complex song on *Pink Moon*, this dates to back to 1968 or possibly earlier. Nick performed it at the Queen Elizabeth Hall in 1969 and it was a strong candidate for inclusion on both his previous albums. Joe Boyd was particularly disappointed that Nick wouldn't record the song for *Bryter Layter*, preferring to include instrumentals. The guitar is in the standard tuning and the lyric is a young, naive take on Nick's regular theme about experimenting with drugs to find out greater truths.

KNOW

With a lyric of just 20 words and a guitar accompaniment played on only two strings (the fifth and sixth at the twelfth fret), this is as bleak as it gets on *Pink Moon*. Unsettling.

RIDE

Also known as Free Ride, the title is a play on the surname of Nick's on-off girlfriend Sophia Ryde. Using a CGCFCE tuning, the song employs the kind of spare lyric Nick was using at the time, more direct than he would have dreamed of a few years earlier.

PARASITE

Another older song, dredged up from the 1969 work tape, this echoes the feeling of alienation in the big city explored in *Bryter Layter*'s At The Chime Of A City Clock and was probably abandoned in favour of it. The reference to 'sailing downstairs to the Northern Line' suggests it was written in Belsize Park close to Chalk Farm tube station, which still has a sign saying 'Stairs to Northern Line'. The tuning is DGDGDF#.

HARVEST BREED

Like several of the songs on *Pink Moon* this sounds unfinished, reminiscent of the works-in-progress to be found on bootleg versions of the work tape. Perhaps Nick was making a point. 'This could just be the end' is surely another reference to early death.

FROM THE MORNING

A deceptively jaunty guitar tuned to CGCFCF accompanies a raw and desolate vision of the future, which includes the lines featured on Nick's headstone: 'now we rise and we are everywhere'. Just 28 minutes after it began Nick's third album is all over.

POSTHUMOUS RELEASES

The 1974 recordings

Until the release of Tow The Line in 2004, these were always known as 'the last four tracks'. Now they are the last five. They first appeared as part of the *Fruit Tree* box and then on the *Time Of No Reply* compilation in 1987. Different takes of two of the songs were released alongside Tow The Line on *Made To Love Magic* in 2004.

RIDER ON THE WHEEL

A pretty guitar accompaniment, DGDGBD, supports a simple lyric in the style of Know and Road from *Pink Moon*. Bootleg recordings of the guitar track only suggest that by 1974 Nick was unwilling or incapable of singing and playing at the same time. On the version that appeared on *Made To Love Magic* in 2004 Nick forgets the words at the beginning of the final verse, but he nails it on the version from *Time Of No Reply* released in 1987 although, by his own high standards, the vocal performance is poor. The lyrics see him as the hamster in a wheel, a victim of the music business.

BLACK EYED DOG

Probably suggested by Winston Churchill's famous description of depression as a black dog, this stark piece played on just three strings is a harrowing listen. Nick's desperation is tangible. His tormented voice is beyond pleading. As the song proceeds his formerly faultless guitar playing is marred by scuffs and scrapes. He's growing old and he wants to go home. The much-bootlegged guitar-only version is as disturbing as anything you'll hear.

HANGING ON A STAR

Using a bizarre AADAAC# tuning, Nick turns his venom on Joe Boyd. In the first version, recorded in February 1974 and included on *Time Of No Reply*, the accompaniment is partly strummed and the vocal polite and deferential. By July that year, on the version from *Made To Love Magic* (2004), the guitar part is picked and taken at a much faster pace, and the vocal is completely overwrought. 'Why do you keep me hanging on a star,' demands Nick, 'when you deem me so high'?

VOICE FROM THE MOUNTAIN

Re-titled Voices on the *Made To Love Magic* compilation this was another song that dated back to at least 1969. Since trying it out on the work tape, Nick had slowed it down to make the effect even more imploring.

TOW THE LINE

The lost track from 1974 picks up the winning and losing theme of some of Nick's early songs and Ross Grainger has said he remembers Nick playing the song at Bunjie's and The Troubadour in 1969 and 1970. An early disenchantment with Joe Boyd may be the inspiration for the lyric, where 'toe' is mis-spelt 'tow', from the old English military expression meaning to follow the rules and do what you're told. On *Made To Love Magic*, John Wood leaves the recording running until we hear Nick put down his guitar for what would turn out to be the last time.

TRACKS OMITTED FROM *FIVE LEAVES LEFT*

TIME OF NO REPLY

Originally recorded in December 1968, the song was omitted from Nick's first album even though it was one of his favourites and had an orchestral arrangement written by Robert Kirby. Kirby has said this was because Nick thought it too similar to The Thoughts Of Mary Jane. The arrangement lay forgotten until 2003, when Kirby recorded it to augment Nick's vocal-and-guitar version, which had emerged as the title track of the first posthumous compilation.

MAGIC

In his own handwritten copy of this song Nick titled it simply Magic, although it had been known as Made To Love Magic at Cambridge and as the even longer I Was Made To Love

Magic when Joe Boyd asked Richard Hewson to add a string part in 1968. Hewson's version surfaced on the *Time Of No Reply* compilation. Kirby's original effort was abandoned because Nick wanted to include just one song on his debut that featured his voice with strings and no guitar, but it was recorded and added to a clean take for the 2004 *Made To Love Magic* album. The lyric is one of Nick's most direct references to lost innocence.

JOEY

Like Betty and Hazey Jane, Joey is another of Nick's mysterious females. The song first appeared on the work tape, where it had a three-line introduction and was then taken at a slow, dreamy pace. In November 1968 it was recorded at Sound Techniques without the intro, with a brisker tempo and with ladles of echo on the guitar. For the *Made To Love Magic* compilation the track was remixed, the echo minimised and the song restored to its natural beauty. It's one of Nick's best tunes but tortuous expressions like 'she wouldn't be there if it could be that you were' caused it to be passed over. This is a pity because the image of the much-loved Joey visiting the singer's grave to see the flowers is a moving one and another insight into Nick's fatalistic take on the world.

CLOTHES OF SAND

Recorded in November 1968, this is one of Nick's earliest and simplest compositions, dating from the summer of 1967 and his trip to Morocco. The lyrics, not least the references to silver spoons and coloured lights, suggest the influence of LSD and other drugs, which he was starting to take around the same time.

MAYFAIR

Some critics have detected the influence of Molly Drake in this gently strummed song about the richest part of central London. But it also sounds like Waterloo Sunset and Penny Lane, songs from an era when English life seemed somehow quaint and lovable. Nick recorded the best version, included on *Made To Love Magic*, on Robert Kirby's reel-to-reel Ferrograph in 1968, but the Sound Techniques version from October that year is notable for the amusing passage where Nick forgets the words and giggles.

OFFICIALLY RELEASED HOME RECORDINGS

BEEN SMOKING TOO LONG

Found on a tape in the Far Leys music room, this was released in 1986 before anyone had claimed authorship. Given the story of Nick's later years, it's a remarkably prescient lyric written in 1966 by Robin Frederick who taught the song to Nick while they were both studying in Aix-en-Provence in 1967. Nick changed the line 'Got the marijuana blues' to 'Got no other life to choose', but retained 'Got a nightmare made of hash dreams'. Robin's website (www.robinfrederick.com) contains more on this song and her relationship with Nick.

STRANGE MEETING II

A hippy-dippy love song about Nick's 'Princess Of The Sand' with a simple and derivative chord progression, the title may carry a reference to Wilfred Owen's poem 'Strange Meeting'.

But Nick also referred to another early song as Strange Meeting I as well as Bird Flew By (see below).

PLAISIR D'AMOUR

A few seconds of Nick playing an instrumental version of this popular 18th-century French melody made famous in the 1960s by Joan Baez and included as a bonus track on the 2004 CD *A Treasury*.

UNOFFICIAL RELEASES

There are many Nick Drake bootlegs in circulation, some of very dubious quality, and all, it must be said, illegally distributed. Many include poorly copied fragments of the so-called 'work tape', in reality several spools of quarter-inch tape recorded by Nick in the music room at Far Leys, containing early versions of Fly, Poor Boy and Joey. This is also the source of Nick's monologue, recorded in 1967. Some bootlegs credit Brian Wells with recording some of the home recordings, but he denies this. Songs from this period that have never been released officially are:

BLOSSOM (FRIEND)
BLUE SEASON
JOEY IN MIND
LEAVING ME BEHIND
MICKEY'S TUNE
(MY LOVE LEFT WITH THE) RAIN
OUTSIDE

STRANGE MEETING I / BIRD FLEW BY
TO THE GARDEN

Collectors can also find copies of Nick's recordings of other people's songs, which date from 1967 and 1968. The influence of the blues and of mid-1960s folk guitarists like Dave van Ronk, Bert Jansch, John Renbourn and Jackson C Frank is clear. The most commonly available tracks are the following.

ALL MY TRIALS
An old Negro spiritual popularised by Peter Paul And Mary, this features a simple calypso-style guitar accompaniment by Nick and a vocal duet with his actress sister Gabrielle Drake.

BLACK MOUNTAIN BLUES
Variously credited to James C Johnson or H Cole, this 12-bar blues was recorded by Bessie Smith in 1930, but Nick heard it on an album he bought in Aix called *Dave Van Ronk Sings Ballads, Blues And A Spiritual*. Van Ronk, who died in 2002, was a popular folk singer on the New York circuit that included Bob Dylan.

BLUES RUN THE GAME
The American folk singer Jackson C Frank, a regular at Les Cousins in the late 1960s, was a big influence on Nick.

Reputedly his first ever composition, he wrote and recorded this in England and it became the title track of his first album in 1965.

COCAINE BLUES

Based on a blues by Luke Jordan from Lynchburg, Virginia, Nick may have heard this on Dave Van Ronk's album *Folk Singer* or perhaps via Robin Frederick in Aix. His rather effete pronunciation of 'cock'-aine instead of 'coke'-aine is faintly risible to modern ears.

COURTING BLUES

Written and recorded by Bert Jansch, this song features on his classic eponymous album released in April 1965, along with Needle Of Death and his version of Davy Graham's Angie.

DON'T THINK TWICE IT'S ALRIGHT

A speeded-up version of the Dylan classic, which first appeared on *The Freewheelin' Bob Dylan* in 1963.

GET TOGETHER

Written by Dino Valenti (often mis-spelt Valente) from The Quicksilver Messenger Service, this slice of US hippy pop was a hit for The Youngbloods featuring Jesse Colin Young, but

Nick's more folky version sounds as though he may have heard Jefferson Airplane's Signe Anderson sing it on their first album *Takes Off* (1966).

HERE COME THE BLUES
Another self-penned track from Jackson C Frank's 1965 album *Blues Run The Game*.
IF YOU LEAVE ME PRETTY MAMA
This traditional blues was included on Dave Van Ronk's *Ballads, Blues And A Spiritual* album and was a staple in 1960s folk clubs.

MILK & HONEY
Another track written and recorded by Jackson C Frank on his 1965 album *Blues Run The Game*.

MY SUGAR SO SWEET
Recorded as My Baby's So Sweet by Dave Van Ronk, this 12-bar blues is a version of Woman, You're So Sweet by the legendary bluesman Blind Boy Fuller.

STROLLING DOWN THE HIGHWAY
Written and recorded by Bert Jansch on his classic eponymous album released in April 1965.

SUMMERTIME
First heard in the 1935 musical *Porgy And Bess*, this famous lyric by Du Bose Heyward for Ira Gershwin's melody has been recorded many times. Nick probably heard it on The Zombies' first album, sung by Colin Blunstone whose breathy delivery and very English vowels have often been compared to Nick's own.

TOMORROW IS SUCH A LONG TIME
Although Bob Dylan's own version of this song didn't appear until 1971 it was widely available on bootlegs throughout the 1960s. Nick may have picked it up in Aix, although he could have heard Elvis Presley's version from 1967.

WINTER IS GONE
A traditional Appalachian song recorded by English folk guitarist John Renbourn, later a member of Pentangle with Bert Jansch and Nick's double bass player Danny Thompson, on his eponymous album released in 1965.

Notes

INTRODUCTION

1   With guitarist Charlie Hunter on his album *Analog Playground* (Blue Note).

2   Now recorded by Hutchings' new band, Rainbow Chasers on *Some Colours Fly* (Talking Elephant).

3   *Poor Boy – Songs of Nick Drake* (Songlines SGL SA4202-2), 2004.

4   Patrick Humphries, *Nick Drake* (Bloomsbury, 1997).

1. CAMBRIDGE

5   Island Records press release for *Five Leaves Left*, September 1969.

6   *The Glittering Prizes*, BBC TV, 1976.

7   Mick Brown, *Sunday Telegraph*, 1997.

8   *Picture This: A Stranger Among Us*, BBC TV, 1998.

9   The grand old building still standing at 7 West Road shows what number 9 would have looked like in Nick's time.

10 From the 1967 movie *Cool Hand Luke*. The redneck prison officer played by Strother Martin says it first. Paul Newman as Luke mocks him with the same line later in the film.

11   Modern British TV viewers will be familiar with David Starkey the historian; in the late 1960s he was one of the leading figures of the right at Fitzwilliam.

2. THE ROUNDHOUSE

12   The date of this gig has been debated for decades. Other writers have placed it in 1968, but we can now be certain that it took place in Christmas week 1967.

13   This is the only report of Nick playing the guitar standing up. Robert Kirby says he always sat down and that his guitars didn't have straps on them.

14   *De Mysterieuze Drake*, VRT Radio 1.

15   Most students at Cambridge, like Nick, are awarded 'a place'. Some, who get particularly high marks in the entrance exam, are given extra cash and better rooms and called 'scholars'. In between are a few students awarded 'an exhibition', a kind of second-class scholarship.

16   A Footlights talent show.

17   Q4 had been occupied by David Frost a few years earlier. Robert's immediate neighbour was Mark Wing-Davey, who went on to play Zaphod Beeblebrox in BBC Radio and TV's *The Hitchhiker's Guide To The Galaxy*

18   Short for Fabulous Cabaret; the notes FABCAB were their signature tune.

19   VRT Radio 1.

20   Quoted by Gabrielle Drake in the Jeroen Berkvens documentary *A Skin Too Few* (2000).

21   Nick's style at this time can be heard on the versions of River Man and Magic that were recorded as demos in Robert Kirby's

room during 1968 and later included on the 2004 CD *Made To Love Magic*.

3. FIVE LEAVES LEFT

22   This former coffee shop is now a branch of Hobbs.

23   Quoted by Gabrielle Drake in *Picture This*, BBC, 1998.

24   Used on the sleeve of the *Fruit Tree* boxed set.

25   Recorded as Angie by Bert Jansch and as Anji by Paul Simon.

26   The mirrored walls of this former 'young gentlemen's club' now house a branch of Pizza Express.

27   Lonmay Old Manse between Fraserburgh and Peterhead; John has recently been awarded three Red Rosettes for his cooking.

28   VRT Radio 1.

29   VRT Radio 1.

30   Their single, Hoots Mon, was number one in 1958.

31   See the Discography for a track-by-track review of *Five Leaves Left*.

32   Morris shot the front cover of *Led Zep 4*.

33   Sharp designed the sleeves for Cream's *Disraeli Gears* and *Wheels On Fire*, and also wrote the lyrics for Cream's Tales Of Brave Ulysses.

34   The factory was demolished in the 1970s and replaced by a housing estate – all that remains is the street name Morgans' Way.

35   VRT Radio 1.

4. EMPIRE

36 A public school in England is of course anything but; the expression means 'a private school' where fees are paid and consequently only children of well-to-do families are admitted.

37 Now officially called Myanmar, though this new name is not recognised by the US or UK Governments; many travel companies boycott the country in protest at human rights abuses by its military regime.

38 For more information on the company see *The Bombay Burmah Trading Corporation Ltd 1863–1963* (Millbrook Press, 1964) by AH Pointon, Rodney Drake's predecessor in the Rangoon office.

39 Now renamed Yangon.

40 A small whisky.

41 Now known as Mumbai.

42 Modern Puné.

43 Father of the prominent democracy campaigner Aung San Suu Kyi, who was awarded the Nobel Peace Prize in 1991 while under house arrest.

5. FAR LEYS

44 Nick Drake: Fruit Tree.

45 Mistakenly called Jack London in Patrick Humphries' 1997 book.

46 Literally 'Miss Manaw'.

47 As we know, the two Karens, Rosie and Ma Naw, hated the Burmese and would have rejected this description; amah is an oriental word for nanny.

48 *De Mysterieuze Drake*, VRT Radio 1.

49 *Lost Boy: In Search Of Nick Drake*, produced by Dave Barber, BBC Radio 2, 1998, updated 2004.

50 *De Mysterieuze Drake*, VRT Radio 1.

51 *De Mysterieuze Drake*, VRT Radio 1.

52 *A Stranger In Our Midst* (1997); *A Skin Too Few* (2000).

53 *Lost Boy: In Search Of Nick Drake.*

6. MARLBOROUGH

54 Artist & Repertoire, basically the record company's talent spotter. Nick Stewart signed U2 to Island in the 1980s.

55 Patrick Humphries, *Nick Drake* (Bloomsbury, 1997).

56 You can take a virtual tour of Marlborough College at www.marlboroughcollege.org.

57 Roughly the equivalent of a modern GCSE exam.

58 University Central Council for Admissions – an application for a university place.

59 A colour is awarded for representing the school in competitive games.

60 Hockey is played by 11 players a side so we can assume that Nick was in the top 22 (XXII in Latin) though not the first 11 (XI).

61 Combined Cadet Force.

62 Quoted by Gabrielle Drake in *Picture This* (BBC TV, 1998).

63 Columbia 33SX 1711.

64 NickDrake.com.

65 In Nick's case East Anglia, Durham, London and Southampton.

7. AIX

66 Fitzwilliam College archives.

67 Quoted by Gabrielle Drake in *Picture This* (BBC TV, 1998).

68 http://www.robinfrederick.com.

69 Although Nick's Monologue, as it has come to be called, is available on many bootleg recordings and has been transcribed by a number of websites, it has never been published officially and cannot be reproduced here for copyright reasons.

8. BRYTER LATER

70 Day Is Done and Way To Blue.

71 Patrick Humphries, *Nick Drake* (Bloomsbury, 1997).

72 247 metres medium wave.

73 £1.25 to 40p.

74 Keith James, who tours the UK with a one-man show called 'The Songs Of Nick Drake', uses three guitars pre-tuned.

75 BBC Radio 2.

76 There was no single taken from the album.

77 Chapman appeared at the November 2004 Nick Drake tribute concert in the old Les Cousins building.

78 This person's name has been changed.

79 Keith Morris, the photographer, has a compelling theory that the reason why Nick's sleeves are so short in all his publicity shots is because he was wearing his father's Turnbull & Asser cast-offs.

80 From Parasite, written in Belsize Park in 1969, released on *Pink Moon* in 1972.

81 Dave Pegg

82 VRT Radio 1.

83 www.john-cale.com.

84 Later Rufus Wainwright's stepfather.

85 The track listing on the white label reads: 'STORMBRINGER (John Martyn), WAY TO BLUE (Nick Drake), GO OUT AND GET IT (John Martyn), WHEN THE DAY IS DONE (Nick Drake), TIME HAS TOLD ME (Nick Drake), SATURDAY SUN (Nick Drake), SWEET HONESTY (Beverly Martyn), YOU GET BRIGHTER (Mike Heron), THIS MOMENT (Mike Heron), I DON'T MIND (Ed Carter), PIED PAUPER (Ed Carter) Lead Vocals: tracks 1–7 by Elton John, tracks 8–11 by Linda Peters.'.

86 Later Nigel's wife, mis-spelt 'Weymouth' on the CD sleeve of *Made To Love Magic*.

87 Fans have assumed that the guitar in the photograph is Nick's own, but it was actually an instrument once owned by Eric Clapton, which was borrowed for the session from *Oz* designer Martin Sharp.

9. PINK MOON

88 Quoted on www.algonet.se/~iguana.

89 www.schizophrenia.com.

90 James Lovelock, *A New Look at Life on Earth* (OUP).

91 VRT Radio 1.

92 VRT Radio 1.

93 BBC, *Picture This*, 1998.

94 You can hear these rare recordings at http://home.hetnet.nl/
~peter.borman/

95 Things Behind The Sun was written in 1968 and featured in
the 1969 Royal Festival Hall gig.

10. BLACK EYED DOG

96 VRT Radio 1.

97 Gorm Henrik Rasmussen, 'Sangeren og guitaristen'.

98 An old concrete garage inside the former Chelsea dairy.

99 Retitled Voices for the 2004 compilation *Made To Love Magic*.

100 'Tow' is Nick's own spelling; he is likely to have meant 'toe
the line'.

11. AFTERMATH

101 Reproduced in Patrick Humphries, *Nick Drake* (Bloomsbury,
1997).

102 Scott Appel reported that Molly and Rodney had told him
that Nick did indeed try to hang himself in 1973 and was cut
down from a beam at Far Leys.

103 Quoted by Patrick Humphries in *Nick Drake* (Bloomsbury,
1997).

104 Kent's piece ended with a wonderful quotation from Neil
Powell's 1978 article in the *London* magazine: 'the listener of
the future will be able to discover from Nick Drake what it
was like in our time to be honest, English and a bit screwed
up'.

105 Patrick Humphries (*Nick Drake*, Bloomsbury, 1997) states
that four tracks from *Pink Moon* were removed to

accommodate the four new songs, but this is not true. The *Pink Moon* disc was simply re-sequenced with eight of the original tracks on side one instead of five.

12. TIME HAS TOLD ME

106 I should admit that I wrote this series and that there was no 'panel of experts' as the newspaper claimed. Nick's album sleeve was the only one of the 100 that *The Times* couldn't find to photograph. They borrowed my copy.

107 The studio in Chelsea had been closed down and sold many years earlier.

108 Published by Forlaget Hovedland in Danish only.

109 The short title was also taken from Nick's own transcription of the lyrics in a notebook.

AFTERWORD

110 Larry Ayres, a Californian who visited the Drakes shortly after Nick's death, wrote to me with an astonishing anecdote about Nick's father, whom he described as having 'pale almost translucent skin', an uncanny parallel with Linda Thompson's description of Nick. Rodney took Ayres into the back garden at Far Leys in 1982 and embarked on a tirade about how his only son would never help with chores. 'For some reason,' wrote Ayres, 'I think that Rodney felt like he had to have the last word in a long-standing argument over doing yard work with his son. I felt as if I was a surrogate Nick to him, or that by telling this to me he was getting even with Nick. It was clear that even though he was restrained in his words, he was seething angry underneath.

He also seemed to get physically very agitated, almost clenching his fists.'

111 See Henry Wallis's famous painting of Chatterton's death at the Tate Gallery or at http://www.victorianweb.org/painting/wallis/paintings/1.html.

Sources

INTERVIEWS

Mike Appleton	BBC TV producer
Larry Ayers	journalist
Dominic Baker-Smith	university director of studies
Ashley Bent	landlord, The Bell, Tanworth
Jeroen Berkvens	Director, A Skin Too Few
Chris Blackwell	Island Records
Joe Boyd	Producer, Manager, Publisher
Chris Bristow	Cambridge supervisor, 1968/9
Mick Brown	journalist
Cally von Callomon	Nick Drake Estate
Iain Cameron	friend, musicologist
Richard Charkin	friend
Joe Cobbe	friend
Tony Cox	musician
Ray Crabtree	Tanworth resident
Jason Creed	editor, Pynk Moon

Simon Crocker	friend
Jonathan Dayton	TV director
Colin Fleetcroft	friend, musician
Pete Frame	journalist
Geoff Frost	designer, Sound Techniques studio
Bruce Fursman	musician
Jerry Gilbert	journalist
Ed Gilchrist	friend
Herman Gilligan	fan
Dr Ross Grainger	friend, musician
Clive Gregson	musician
Rev Tim Harmer	Tanworth vicar
Roy Harper	musician
Charlie Hart	musician
Alex Henderson	friend
Andrew Hicks	friend
Robyn Hitchcock	musician
Patrick Humphries	writer/biographer
Ashley Hutchings	musician
Gilbert Isbin	musician
Keith James	musician
Sir Elton John	musician
Dr. Ray Kelly	Fitzwilliam College tutor
Randall Keynes	friend
Robert Kirby	friend, arranger

Joe Levy	journalist, Rolling Stone
Julian Lloyd	friend
Jeremy Mason	friend
Keith Morris	photographer
Andrew Murison	friend
Denise Offringa	fan
Rob Partridge	Island PR
Peter Paphides	journalist
Mark Pavey	fan, musician
Dave Pegg	musician
Mike Petty	historian
Prof. David Punter	friend
Gorm Henrik Rasmussen	biographer
Tony Reif	producer
Peter Rice	recording engineer
Sophia Ryde	friend
John Saunders	friend
Mike Schutzer-Weissman	friend
Dennis Silk	Marlborough College housemaster
Robert Smith	musician, The Cure
Nick Stewart	Island A&R man
Linda Thompson	friend
John Venning	friend
Stuart Villaroel	fan, musician
Dr Brian Wells	friend, addiction counsellor

Paul Wheeler   friend, musician

Muff Winwood   Island A&R

BOOKS

Humphries, Patrick: *Nick Drake* (Bloomsbury 1997)

Rasmussen, Gorm Henrik: *Pink Moon - Sangeren og guitaristenNick Drake* (Forlaget Hovedland, 1980)

ARTICLES

Brown, Mick: 'The Sad Ballad of Nick Drake' (*Sunday Telegraph*,1997)

Gilbert, Jerry: 'Something Else For Nick?' (*Sounds*, 1971)

Hicks, Andrew: 'Nick Drake - A Memoir of My Childhood Friend' (Bryter Music, 2000)

Kent, Nick: 'Songs of Waving, Drowning & A Sort of Sadness' (unpublished, 1979)

Kornelussen, Frank: Sleeve Notes for *Time of No Reply* (Hannibal Records, 1986)

Lubow, Arthur: Sleeve notes for *Fruit Tree* (Island Records, 1979)

McKnight, Connor: 'In Search of Nick Drake' (*Zigzag*, 1974)

Paphides, Peter: 'Stranger To The World' (*Observer*, 2004)

WEBSITES

Bryter Dayes – www.bryterdayes.org
Bryter Music (the estate of Nick Drake) – www.brytermusic.com
Iain Cameron's Diary – /icameron.diaryland.com/older.html
La Luna Rosa (Italian) – www.lalunarosa.com
Made To Love Magic – www.geocities.com/made2lovemagic
Michael Organ – www.michaelorgan.au/list/htm
Nick Drake.com – www.nickdrake.com
Robin Frederick – www.robinfrederick.com/index.html
Rock's Back Pages – www.rocksbackpages.com
Schizophrenia.com – www.schizophrenia.com/index.html
The Nick Drake Files – www.algonet.se/~iguana/DRAKE/DRAKE.html

TV / RADIO

Picture This: A Stranger Among Us (dir: Tim Clements; BBC TV, 1998)

Fruit Tree: The Nick Drake Story (prod: David Barber, BBC Radio 2, 1998)

A Skin Too Few (dir: Jeroen Berkvens; Humanist Broadcasting Foundation, 2000)

Lost Boy: In Search of Nick Drake (prod: David Barber; BBC Radio 2, 2004)

De Mysterieuze Drake (VRT Radio 1, 2004)

Index